AF575966

ALSO BY PAUL MARION

POETRY

Lockdown Letters & Other Poems

Union River: Poems and Sketches

NONFICTION

Portraits Along the Way: 1976-2024

Mill Power: The Origin and Impact of Lowell National Historical Park

CO-AUTHOR

French Class: French Canadian-American Writings on Identity, Culture, and Place with Susan April, Paul Brouillette, and Marie Louise St. Onge

EDITOR

Atop an Underwood: Early Stories and Other Writings by Jack Kerouac

CO-EDITOR

Atlantic Currents: Connecting Cork and Lowell
with Tina Neylon and John Wooding

History as It Happens: Citizen Bloggers in Lowell, Mass.
with Richard P. Howe Jr.

City Hikes

Field Notes

City Hikes

Field Notes

PAUL MARION

LP

Loom Press
Amesbury, Massachusetts
2025

City Hikes: *Field Notes*

www.paulmarion.com

ISBN 978-0-931507-55-7

Printed in the United States of America
First edition
Design: Keith Finch
Printing: Versa Press, Illinois
Author photograph: Tony Sampas
Lowell Walks photographs: Richard P. Howe Jr., Roxane Howe, & Joseph Marion
Map of Lowell, Mass: Library of Congress
Text: Garamond

Loom Press
15 Atlantic View, Amesbury, MA 01913
www.loompress.com
info@loompress.com

Many of these compositions first appeared on the *RichardHowe.com* and *PaulMarion.com* blogs. "Batman on Highland Street," "Scenes from a Redevelopment Zone," and "Grand Street Peace Walk" were reprinted in *History as It Happens: Citizen Bloggers in Lowell, Mass.* "Watching the Canalway" appears in *Mill Power: The Origin and Impact of Lowell National Historical Park.* "Merrimack Street" and "Labor Day Eve" were published in *Strong Place: Poems '74-'84.* "A Higher Level of Notation," which first appeared in the poetry collection *Middle Distance,* was commissioned in 1986 by the Lowell Sesquicentennial Committee for the 150th anniversary of the incorporation of Lowell, Massachusetts.

Special thanks to Richard P. Howe Jr. for his overview of the successful Lowell Walks public program (2015-2020), which appears as an appendix including a chronology of the series, list of theme walks and guest presenters, and recognition of community partners such as Lowell National Historical Park.

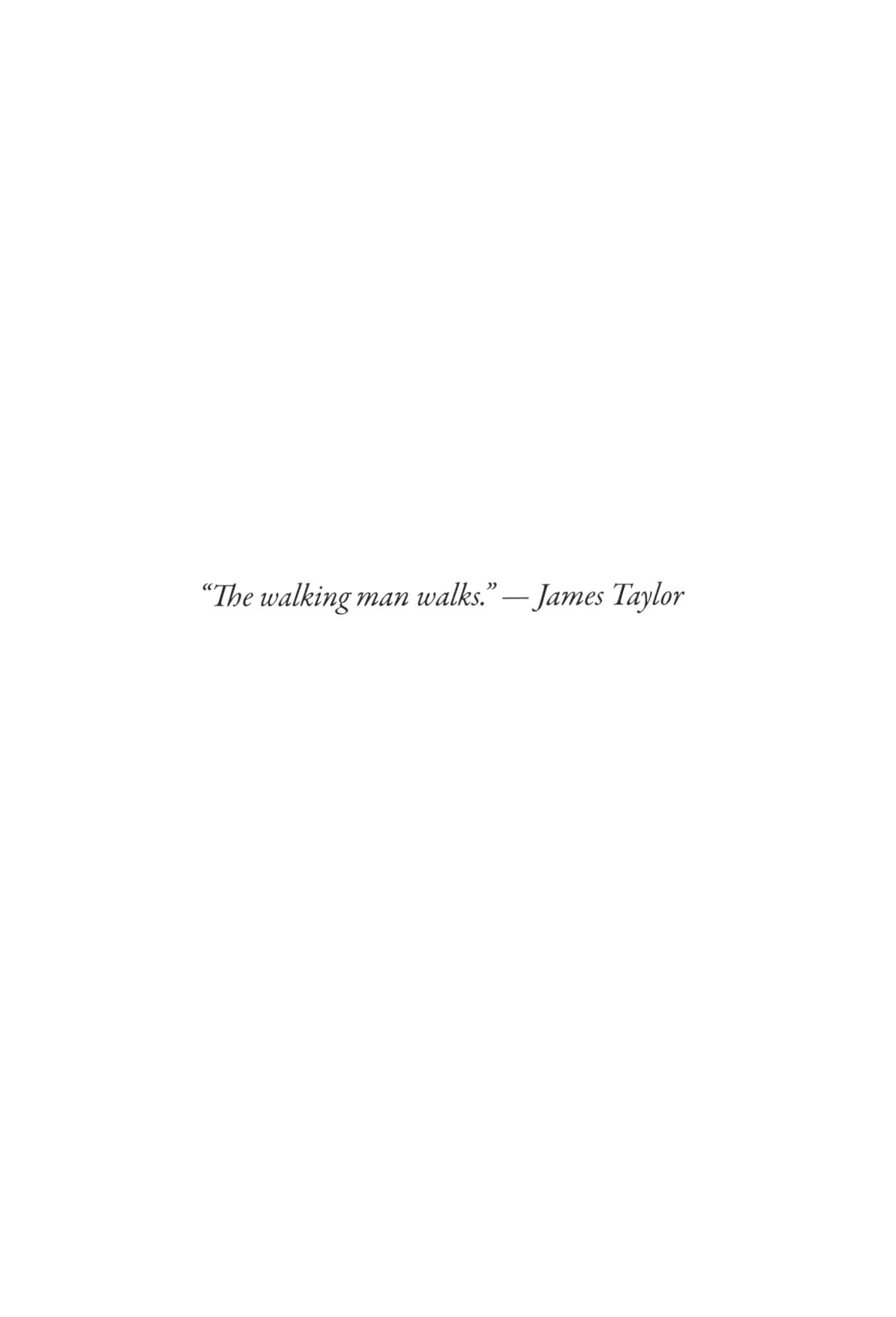

"The walking man walks." — James Taylor

Contents

Introduction

Most of these sketches were written when I returned home after regular Sunday walks between 2009 and 2011. At the time, my family lived on historic Highland Street near the train station in Lowell, Massachusetts, on the border of the South Common and at the edge of downtown. Many fresh reports appeared on the popular *RichardHowe.com* blog in Lowell.

Sometimes I had companions, but usually I walked alone, carrying a notebook and pen. I would go out for an hour or two. I wanted to see what I could see and listen more closely to life on the streets that were familiar to me or in other places I only knew by driving through. A few pieces in this collection, written earlier as free verse poems, are included in prose form to show that walking in the city has long interested me.

Also included here is the text of my part of a panel discussion about the post-American city at an American Studies conference in Lowell in 2009. Through the lens of my walking experiences, I pictured "change over time" in Lowell as a prototypical early industrial city now in a later stage of development. No longer the traditional urban center of its past, essentially an ethnic factory city for decades, Lowell is socially and economically "new," a place adapting to internal and external influences—regional, national, and global. The demographics, economic mix (technology and knowledge sectors), views on land use and architectural preservation, and more have evolved. A place adapting, yes, but also altering our understanding of a mid-sized city in the twenty-first century.

I haven't been the only one walking around. After the account of my walks, readers will find an appendix with details about the popular Lowell Walks public program initiated by Richard P. Howe Jr. in 2015. Through 2020 and continuing with the National Park Service (NPS), summers have been animated by a series of guided tours in the city led by Dick Howe Jr., various guest guides, and the NPS. The topics ranged from trains & trolleys to abolitionism and from public art to downtown fires. The ninety-minute tours averaged one hundred walkers and as many as two hundred a few times.

The initiative was an experiment based on what Dick had seen for several years in leading guided tours at the Lowell Cemetery. He was convinced there is a local audience for encounters with other aspects of the city's history and notable figures. The response proved he was correct. Since the establishment of a national historical park in 1978, the public has been offered Park Ranger-led tours about the power canals, women mill workers, immigrant neighborhoods, and architecture. Lowell Walks expanded the menu with new subject matter and community experts. —PM

City Hikes: *Field Notes*

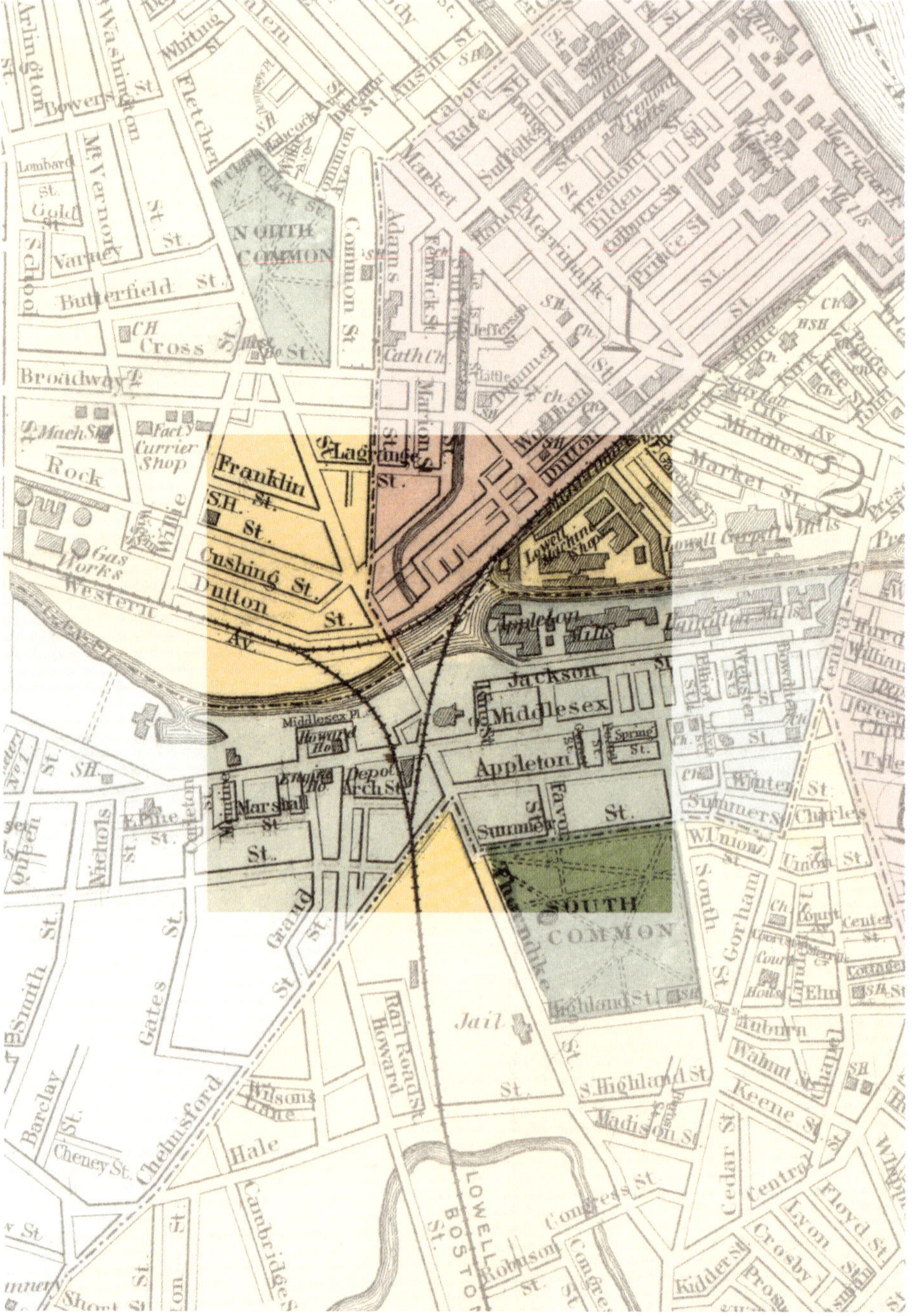

Arlington St.
Washington St.
Whiting St.
Bowers St.
Fletcher St.
Mt Vernon St.
Lombard St.
Gold St.
School St.
Varney St.
Butterfield St.
NORTH COMMON
Common St.
Cross St.
Broadway
Austin St.
Cabot St.
Race St.
Market St.
Suffolk St.
Tremont St.
Tremont Mills
Tilden St.
Prince St.
Merrimack St.
Adams St.
Fenwick St.
Jefferson
Cath Ch.
Marion St.
Lagrange St.
Dutton St.
Franklin St.
Cushing St.
Dutton St.
Western Av.
Rock St.
Currier Shop
Gas Works
Lowell Machine Shop
Lowell Carpet Mills
Market St.
Middlesex St.
City Hall
Appleton Mills
Hamilton Mills
Jackson St.
Middlesex St.
Middlesex Pl.
Howard
Depot
Arch St.
Marshall St.
Appleton St.
Favor St.
Spring St.
Summer St.
Winter St.
Charles St.
Union St.
Nichols St.
E. Pine St.
SOUTH COMMON
Thorndike St.
Highland St.
South St.
Gorham St.
Court St.
Center St.
Elm St.
Jail
Grand St.
Gates St.
Smith St.
Barclay St.
Cheney St.
Chelmsford St.
Wilsons Lane
Hale St.
Howard St.
Rail Road St.
S. Highland St.
Madison St.
Auburn St.
Walnut St.
Keene St.
Cedar St.
Central St.
Floyd St.
Lyon St.
Crosby St.
Kidder St.
Congress St.
Robinson St.
Cambridge St.
Short St.
LOWELL BOSTON

Crayon Mill

My brother and I made the rounds downtown this morning to get some fresh air and work out the winter kinks. The sky was a pure powder-blue backdrop behind the brick buildings. We started at Broadway and Dutton. Near the Swamp Locks boat landing of the National Park Service, we were intrigued by what looked like a large rectangular white tent that turned out to be a construction site. Walking around the back side, we saw that the wind had whipped off sections of a plastic tarp, revealing scaffolding around two ancient wooden lock-chamber gates, as best as we could guess. Mounted on frames, the gates appear to be undergoing restoration.

With the fence open at the small canal bridge, we hiked on through the Hamilton Canal District and down Jackson Street. I hadn't noticed until today that someone had chipped off the letters spelling HAMILTON from one of the stone arches, right next to another one with the date of the mill's origin, 1825, still in fine condition. The air was chilly at 9 a.m., so as much as possible we walked on the sun-washed side of the street. The stretch of the Pawtucket Canal leading from the Doubletree Hotel towards the Swamp Locks is informally known as the "Industrial Canyon," but a walker also gets the sense of being in an industrial canyon when passing through the Hamilton complex and under the remaining elevated "Jackson Properties" walkway. We saw a few people heading somewhere. It was too cold for the seagulls—or too early.

My brother noted that the Major's Pub building was once a painters' union hall. The structure has character, featuring details such as a metal roof. The same goes for the small outcropping entryway section of the mill across the street. It looks like a piece of a canal gatehouse. You see it on your left when walking down the driveway toward the "Lofts" apartments, one of the city's better mill conversions. My brother said the gatehouse reminded him of the tiny "crayon mill" that once stood near what is now the Fred C. Church Insurance building off French Street opposite Lucy Larcom Park. He said it housed a manufacturer of crayons and chalk at one time—items used to mark fabric in the mills.

We turned down Central Street, which needs a major retail upgrade on the west side and slipped through the tunnel off Prescott Street to see where the new cheese-and-wine shop is set to open, facing the canal and hotel. The in-progress interior is impressive with its shelves, furnishings, and raw stone wall. Good luck to "Ricardo" with his venture. Let's hope the Canalway-front business approach catches on. Our next stop was Kerouac Park, just emerging from the December-January glacier. The *Kerouac Commemorative* is halfway through its twenty-first year and holding up well. The steel-and-granite benches need repair, and parts of the plaza that have heaved up in recent winters will require leveling. The sculpture area needs a landscaping overhaul. For an international attraction, the plantings should look as good as Kittredge Park in the Belvidere neighborhood.

We took a left on Bridge Street, where Eleni's dress-and-tailoring shop looks sharp as does the travel agency on the corner, Gomes Travel. For all her talents in sewing, gardening, writing, and cooking, Eleni has made a name for herself downtown due to her impromptu "hammocking" as she hooks up her favorite hammock to whatever poles and uprights that she picks out when it's time for a short rest out of the way like an inventive off-roader. Our last long leg was up Merrimack to Shattuck and over the train tracks to the Club Diner for breakfast. By then the sun was high and warm. Sunday customers buzzed in the diner, scarfing up French toast and scrambled eggs and slugging down coffee amid the folded newspapers and eager talk.

February 15, 2009

NORTH COMMON
Common St.
Common Av.
Adams
Fenwick St.
Jefferson
Cath Ch.
Marion St.
Lagrange St.
Franklin St.
Cushing St.
Dutton St.
Western Av.
Gas Works
Rock
Curier Shop
Fact'y
Mach Shop
Broadway
Cross St.
Butterfield St.
School
Varney
Gold
Lombard
Mt Vernon St.
Mt Washington St.
Arlington
Bowers St.
Fletcher
Whiting St.
Dane St.
Gage
Salem
James
Tucker St.
Moody
Ford St.
Aiken
Austin
Hall
Perkins
Cheever
Coolidge St.
Cabot St.
Market St.
Race
Suffolk
Tremont
Tilden
Colburn St.
Prince
Dummer
Little
Worthen
Lowell Machine Shop
Lowell Carpet Mills
Merrimack Mills
Appleton Mills
Hamilton Mills
Jackson St.
Middlesex
Middlesex Pl.
Howard Ho.
Depot
Arch St.
Marsh St.
E. Pine
Nichols
Appleton St.
Summer St.
Spring St.
Winter St.
Summers St.
Charles
Union St.
W. Union
SOUTH COMMON
Thorndike
Highland St.
S. Highland St.
Jail
South St.
Gorham St.
Center St.
Court
Elm St.
Cottage
Auburn
Walnut St.
Grand St.
Gates St.
Smith St.
Rail Road
Howard
Wilsons
Central
Middle St.
City Av.
Kirk
Lee St.
John
Anne
Prescott
Hurd St.
William
Tyler
Church

Acre Passage

I had a seasoned walking partner this morning as we made our way from downtown west up Merrimack Street. The weather was end-of-winter mild, but still cold enough to keep the ice set on sidewalks. Although precipitation was forecast, a mix of snow and rain, the sky held its blank look. We passed City Hall and the public library, which act as civic counterweights to the Auditorium on East Merrimack and mark one edge of the central business district. Watching a TV news report about President Obama's visit to Ottawa earlier this week, I noticed a resemblance between Lowell City Hall and the central tower of the Parliament building in Canada. Another observation from TV popped into my head as we passed the small shops, restaurants, and offices of upper Merrimack. I had just seen a program about food in Ireland that lavished attention on the Irish scene. In big cities and small towns owners paint their shops and pubs in bright colors and hang distinctive signs. Lowell's downtown core has some impressive storefronts, restaurant façades, and well-designed signs. We need to spread the look.

For-sale banners draped the fronts of the former St. Jean Baptiste/*Nuestra Señora del Carmen* church and St. Joseph's Hall across the street. It was good to see the Father Garin statue in place outside the former church. Other than a couple of 1970s-era murals, the area doesn't have much public art for uplift. (On the return leg of our walk, we swung past Harmony Park near St. Patrick Church. The Revolving Museum team and neighborhood friends have done a lot to reclaim the small park, restoring the tile mosaic and adding elements like a wooden figurative sculpture and the temporary ball wall made of soccer balls, basketballs, tennis balls, footballs, and other balls rescued from the canals.)

But back to the church complex—a dramatic example of how cities change over time. In 1896, the 19,000-member parish was the largest French Canadian-American parish in the Archdiocese of Boston. With his fellow Oblate priest Lucien Lagier, Andre Marie Garin had begun his work in Lowell with a mission for French-speaking Catholics in the basement of St. Patrick Church in 1868, when the Franco population was less than 1,500. (Thanks to historian Richard Santerre for these facts.)

We meandered through to Salem Street via the passageway at the former St. Joseph's Hospital (later the Holden Center) and tried to get over to Fletcher Street through the old hospital parking lot only to find ourselves fenced in. It did give us a great view of a stand-out mint-green house on the side street that we wound up taking to get to Fletcher. We proceeded along the North Common, passing the small shop with the sign DONUTS STEAMED DOGS, which neither of us had ever entered. Anyone walking around the city will be struck by the number of small businesses and how many of them are untried by a typical resident. There's a barber shop on Market Street that could be relocated as is to a history museum for the quality of its interior design. The walls are a phenomenal record of Americana, local and national, with a strong Frank Sinatra thread. The images on the walls make the place a time machine.

Any northeast city looks gritty by the end of February. We've had a harsh winter. Outside some pubs the snow has melted to reveal months of cigarette butts. Shrinking icy snowbanks are rimmed in black from car exhaust. Plastic bags decorate bare trees. We're on the verge of mud season. Even on a gray day the gold dome of Holy Trinity church, Greek Orthodox, shines out of the middle of the Acre.

February 22, 2009

Lemieux Park and O'Keefe Circle

Anticipating snow on Sunday after hearing the excited meteorologists for the past few days, I headed off on my own Saturday morning to see what I would find nearby in the Back Central neighborhood. I'd like to make a motion to change the name from Back Central to the Garden District in recognition of the widespread commitment to cultivating flowers, vegetables, and fruits in the neighborhood. This area has a distinctive character, a cultural texture that should be preserved and promoted. There are three names associated with this section of the city or parts of this section: the Flats, the South End, and Back Central. I don't think any one of them captures the feeling of the place. I suggested the name change to the M.I.T. urban planning students whom City planners brought in last fall to collaborate with residents in rethinking the way the neighborhood looks and functions. I hope the idea is still on the table.

A spotless blue sky made a pure dome over the city yesterday morning. It didn't feel as if a storm was due in twenty-four hours. On Elm Street a crowd of small brown birds, maybe sparrows, cheeped like crazy in the hedge outside a two-family house. Pigeons wheeled onto the roof of the original courthouse. I dodged the muddy driveway craters and potholes left from winter's assault. The general look of the area was one of aftermath. Scattered Santas and reindeer stood off to the side of porches, defrosting trash plastered sidewalks, blizzard-shredded flags hung slack, and frost-killed stalks of plants leaned over. The religious yard art, Sacred Heart shrines and bathtub crèche scenes, had weathered the cold months well. The mild air drew neighbors outside for over-the-fence conversations. I wasn't the only walker. Traffic picked up by the quarter hour.

Whenever I walk in this area, I stop at a vest-pocket park that sits between Mill and Richmond streets, Walter J. Lemieux Park, just off Hosford Square. About ten years ago, Back Central neighborhood activists sparked a number of improvements, from car condos on empty lots for more parking to redesigned intersections and new green spaces. With its neat landscaping, flowering trees, white fence, flagpoles, and stone marker, Lemieux Park adds a deeply personal place to the neighborhood. Here, the community honors its own. The text on the memorial stone reads: "In Memory Of/U.S. Army Medic Walter J. Lemieux, SP4/Killed In The Line Of Duty In Vietnam/A Lifelong Resident Of 21 Mill Street/September 23, 1947-March 9, 1969/Dedicated On September 27, 1998." He was twenty-one. Flanked by reddish bushes, the granite marker is about three feet high, finished on the sides. The 10 a.m. sun shone on the face of the monument. Mica flecks in the gray, rough-cut top surface gleamed like starry specks in a patch of the universe.

Half a block away, in the center of a mini-park traffic island in the middle of Hosford Square, there's another memorial marker that can only be appreciated on foot. O'Keefe Circle has an aged bronze plaque set in a large square block of granite. The words on this memorial read: "In Memory Of/John Joseph O'Keefe/Private in U.S. Army/Born August 14, 1883 -/Died September 23, 1932/Enlisted October 13, 1917/Discharged March 28, 1919." A veteran of "The War to End All Wars." This monument once included a vintage machine gun on a tripod. As a boy, I noticed every time we drove through the square.

Around these public remembrances community life perks in its daily rounds: Alpha Insurance Agency, Angelina's Moneygrams, Sprint Phone, G & I Latino Market (*O Brasil mais perto de voce*), Express Tax Services (*imposto de reda*), LP International Store (specialists in imported and local clothes), Luxu's Jewelry Repair, Hair Tech (grand opening), Maranatha Church (The Lord Jesus is Coming), General Practice (immigration/criminal/auto accidents/divorce—*Falamos Portugues, Hablamos Espanol*), P & L Auto Body, and the Language Center (English, Portuguese, Spanish, Computer).

From that busy intersection, I took a side route down to Lawrence Street, past the Whipple Cafe, Bar & Grill at Lawrence and Wamesit streets, and over to the Concord River and Jollene Dubner Park, another tribute that deserves a longer commentary later. Jollene was an environmental activist in the community when the term "Green" was not as common as it is today. The river filled the channel and flowed to the Merrimack, sun dappling the blue-black surface. Northward, around the bend, white foam kicked up over the rocks. In his essay "Walking," Henry David Thoreau writes: "Half the walk is but retracing our steps." Heading back, I passed the last of the red holiday bows on windows and looked hard to see any sign of green in the serpentine grapevines all twisted through the pipe-grids of arbors in the yards. What was on the air at this hour on the micro-radio station broadcasting from a house at the corner of Central and Elm?—1570 AM WKNM, Radio Commercial, *24 Horas Por Dia* Lowell. A runner plugged into his white wires of iTunes breezed by me. A blue-and-red flashing cruiser sped toward downtown. Old Thoreau answered, "I have traveled widely in Concord," when asked by someone why he had not yet visited Europe.

March 1, 2009

Centralville of the Universe

My Sunday walking companion this week was a university historian from Christian Hill who has embraced the city full-strength since moving here about four years ago. We rendezvoused in front of Vic's (Breakfast, Subs & Bakery) at Lilley Ave. and West Sixth Street. Across the street the Lowell Provision Co. (est. 1915), known for its longhorn steer logo, advertised "Our own corned beef homemade red or gray" next to the leprechauns in the front window. Other signs pushed "Italian Sausage Hot or Sweet," "Delicious Prepared Meals," and "Steak and Chicken Marinades." A couple of doors up on West Sixth, towards the Peter J. Deschene Memorial Fire Station, there are the Soap Box Laundry, Nana's American Store (African clothing, cosmetics, and handbags), and Sunrise Scrubs Boutique. Opposite is *La Reneita* Market and Restaurant (Pay your bills here/*Paque sus quentas aqui*) with "Spanish and American food," Michelle's Hair Salon, and Nails by Christina. *Peniel* Spanish Christian Church welcomes worshippers at the corner of Ennell and W. Sixth.

Across the intersection where Aiken Avenue angles in I saw the red, yellow, and green African continent logo of Auntie Rosie's Cultural Market (African and West Indian foods, clothes, and jewelry.) The neighborhood branch of Eastern Bank fills a silver cube between these small businesses and others lined along Lakeview Avenue. In the distance stands A. G. (Ace) Hardware. Every neighborhood has these clusters of small and tiny businesses, most of them owned I assume by residents who depend on the local patrons for earnings with which they pay the rent or mortgage, buy supplies and merchandise, make goods to sell, provide services, hire workers, etc. The Great Recession is changing their lives day by day.

This being Jack Kerouac;s birthday week, we walked northwest up Lakeview Ave. to make a pilgrimage to his birthplace at 9 Lupine Road, the small two-story brown house close to the corner of Orleans Street, which rises sharply and was a favorite sledding hill when my brothers were young. We lived for a while at 67 Orleans before my father used his G.I. benefits to buy a small ranch-style home in the outer Navy Yard section of Dracut. Many of the French-Canadian Americans from *St. Louis de France* parish made the leap to suburbia in the 1950s. *Ste. Thérèse* parish up Lakeview Ave. was an ethnic and religious overflow from *St. Louis de France* parish. The family names matched in the Sunday Mass bulletins.

The top of Orleans offers a panoramic view of the city, especially when the trees are bare. Down the other side, we took Hildreth Street to the east and stopped at the old cemetery near Aiken Ave. The gate to the main section was open, so we looked around. The adjoining Hildreth family cemetery, which includes the imposing gray monument for Benjamin F. Butler (lawyer, industrialist, Civil War general, governor), was locked as usual. Gravestones are like fading photographs. The earliest one I saw was 1810. Many of the names are venerable names from Dracut, which was settled in the mid-1600s and incorporated in 1701. Coburn. Fox. There was an area of Peabody graves, not a name I associate with Greater Lowell. A handful show up in the phonebook. Several markers were broken, but the cemetery is in good shape for its age.

We moved on and took a right that brought us to Homestead Road, which has a few distinctive compact houses that remind me of the small "gingerbread" Victorians in Oak Bluffs on Martha's Vineyard. These houses in Centralville are architectural curiosities, built as worker housing. We wound our way down Bunker Hill Street with its neat houses in a row and on past the shuttered *St. Louis de France* church. My companion lamented the loss of such churches whose activities once stabilized and pumped energy into the community. Today's *Boston Globe* article about the decreasing number of Catholics in Massachusetts underscores the changes.

We moved deeper into the side streets and byways, but that's for another report. In ninety minutes, we covered a broad patch of a neighborhood that is in transition, a place remaking itself house by home, street by block. One pattern is the change from owner-occupied homes to rental properties and new owners. The older generation passes away, and offspring have gone to the suburbs, not interested in the "old country." My mother and her brothers and sisters grew up in Centralville—not one of my twenty cousins from those families stayed in Lowell. Multiply this situation by thousands. If every picture tells a story, in the words of the Rod Stewart song, then every window frames a drama. I think about that when I pass the buildings, each a container packed with history.

March 9, 2009

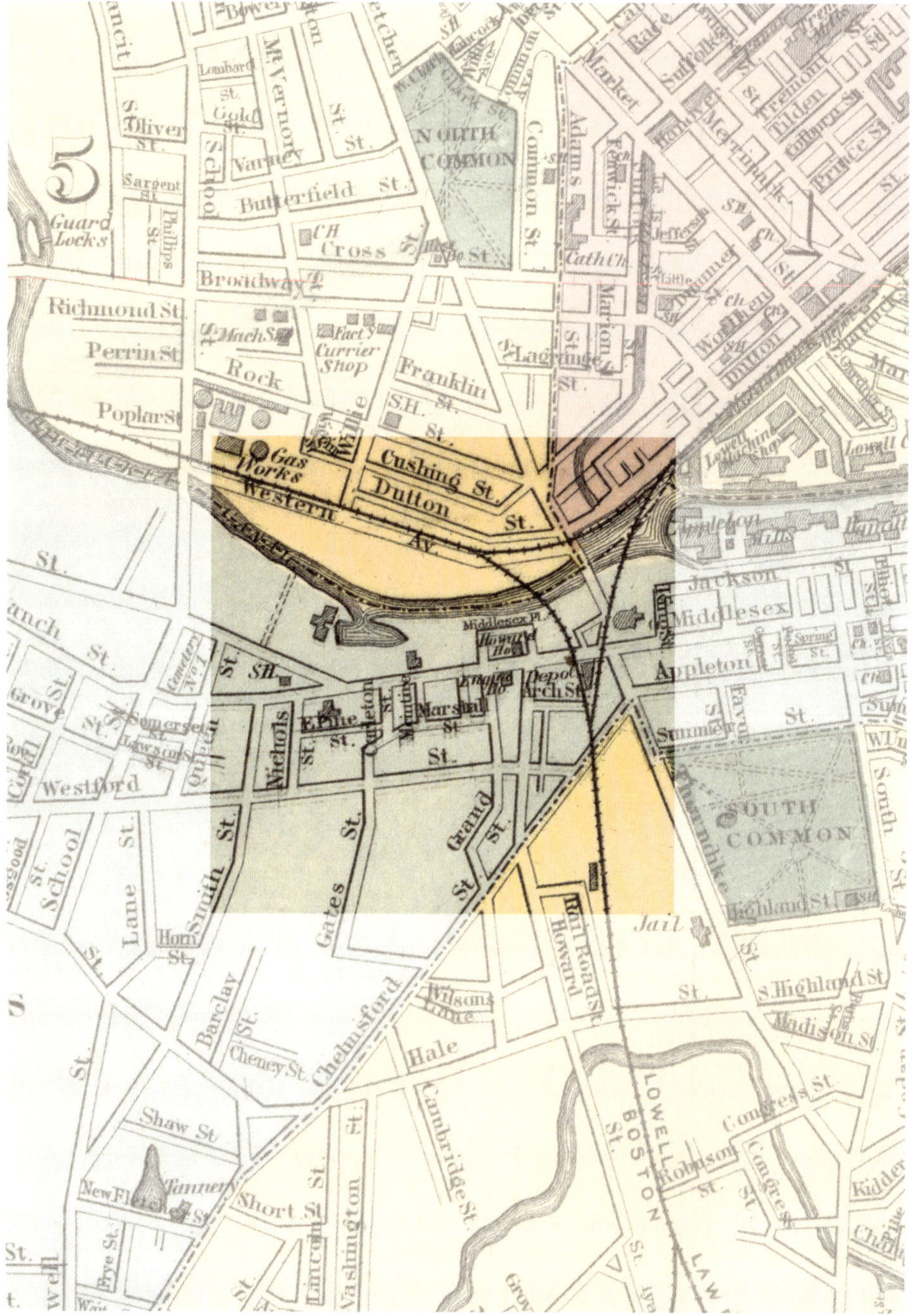

Watching the Canalway

We had a pure blue near-spring morning for a Sunday hike that loosely traced the rough cut of a stretch of canal walkway along the mid-section of the Pawtucket Canal. My walking-partner this morning was the national park superintendent who has expert knowledge of the Canalway, the official name of the system of canal-side paths that crisscross the city. We met on Jackson Street and traversed the Hamilton Canal District, where commercial and residential construction may start by early summer. There's a terrific, mini-industrial canyon vista up the Hamilton Canal with two remaining suspended walkways over the water. The area was quiet at 8 a.m., with the Charter School not in session and the upper-story residents getting a slow start on Sunday. Photographer Jim Higgins calls this area the "last frontier" of Lowell's mill-scape. Once redevelopment begins, changes will come fast. Thankfully, the plan calls for lots of preservation and adaptive reuse—and even the protection of some of the factory ruins as architectural evidence of the scale of production once seen in this part of the city. These are the early mills: Hamilton Mfg. Co. (1825), Appleton Co. (1828).

We walked over the Lord Overpass above Thorndike St. and crossed the invisible line between the Acre and the Lower Highlands. The sidewalk overlooks a subterranean section of Middlesex Street that you have to be looking for not to miss. Of note is the Nobis (sustainable) Engineering building, an historic rehab of the former Davis & Sargent Lumber Co.—this is being certified by the U.S. Green Bldg. Council as a Leadership in Energy and Environmental Design (LEED) project and may be the first LEED project in Lowell. Around the back there is a peculiar chimney, and the side closest to the Boys and Girls

Club is clad in corrugated metal that complements the cleaned-up brick and stone exterior of the original structure. The property backs up to what will be the Canalway path. Birds sang loudly in the trees. Next door is Kenny's Cleaners (leather and suede service center) in a brick building with weathered green window bays that jut out and a stone archway above the door. Behind the Boys and Girls Club back lot is a section of jungle-thick brush so dense it makes a wall of twisted thickets and branches. I don't know what is growing there but it could hide any kind of wildlife.

We popped out around the side of the Club, opposite *Pailin* Plaza with its Asian angles and busy business cluster (*Angkor Wat* Realty, New *Pailin* Jewelry, White Rose Restaurant, H & R Block, etc.). Clemente Park was unusually deserted—it has to be one of the most active parks in the city: basketball, skateboarding, volleyball, swings. The California poet Tom Clark wrote two memorable poems about the baseball legend Roberto Clemente. One short one goes: "won't forget/his nervous/habit of/rearing his/head back/on his neck/like a/proud horse." Another one is about Clemente's death in a plane crash at sea (near the so-called Bermuda Triangle) while on his way to deliver disaster relief supplies to earthquake victims in Nicaragua in 1972. The poem is called "The Great One" and concludes: "No matter how many times/Manny Sanguillen/dove for your body/the sun kept going down/on his inability to find it//I just hope those Martians realize/they are claiming the rights to/far and away the greatest rightfielder/of all time."

At this point, the Pawtucket Canal makes a broad curve around Western Avenue on the other bank. In the early days of the National Park, tourists in the canal boats swinging up this way would often get waves from the workers in the Joan Fabrics plant when the windows were open in the summer.

Past the park we slid down a side street (Saunders) that dead-ends at the canal, where there's a big old taxi barn for yellow cabs, and proceeded down Payne, where you begin to think that Lowell is the auto-body-repair-shop capital of the northeast. We've got Le's and Vo's and M & R and James Trinity bunched up. At the corner is School Street Light Truck Parts, a compact operation. Cabs and back ends are stacked three high just like the shelves of boats at Hampton Beach marina. A green canopy covers a row of tires. We noticed a funny juxtaposition of businesses in the building—upstairs are a chiropractor and a sign about accident treatment. We crossed the Korean War Veterans (School St.) Bridge and passed through the National Grid complex behind the Stoklosa School. When I was a kid, my father would drive our family over the previous School Street bridge late on Sunday afternoons to get fresh, warm donuts from Eat-a-Donut farther down on School, and we'd eat in the car. Nothing beat the marshmallow-filled donuts dusted with powdered sugar. I recall the huge gas tanks right there on School Street—three reddish brown multi-story behemoths, an ominous sight.

We wound our way back up Willie and Franklin streets, where there are two remarkable small stone houses on either side of a wooden house with an unusual roof detail that reads "1902." From there, we picked our way back to the recently completed section of the Canalway along the Western Canal at Suffolk Street, behind the American Textile History Museum, and then crossed Dutton to the Swamp Locks area and back to our starting point. The ice had not completely given up its hold on the canals, and we were surprised to see a battered blue rowboat trapped in the lower part of the Merrimack Canal. How did it get in there?

March 15, 2009

LOWELL
HIGHLANDS
4
Branch St.
Westford
Liberty
Hastings
Osgood St.
School St.
Dover St.
Grove St.
Somerset St.
Nichols St.
Chelmsford
Barclay St.
Cheney St.
Shaw St.
New Fletcher St.
Tannery
Short St.
Lincoln St.
Washington St.
Powell
B. St.
A. St.
Frye St.
Waite St.
Angle St.
Waterloo St.
Manufacturers
Hale
Cambridge St.
Gates St.
Smith St.
Grand St.
Lane St.
Horn St.
Wilsons Lane
Howard Rail Road St.
AYER'S CITY
Canada
Poplar St.
Lincoln
Waldo
Cook
Montreal
Plain
Eaton
Border St.
Old Middlesex
LOWELL
River Meadow Brook
Forrest St.
Middlesex Pl.
Howard Ho.
Depot
Arch St.

Bangkok Market

Last Saturday, I stopped at the Bangkok Market on the corner of Chelmsford and Sheldon streets. It was a little early in the season for their impressive outdoor produce display, a mini version of Boston's Haymarket in the Highlands, but there were lots of Asian vegetables whose names I don't know, along with cartons of grapefruits shining like yellow softballs and trays of green grapes and limes (3/$1.00).

To the right of the entrance on the Sheldon St. side, the store wall serves as a community bulletin board. Two colorful posters promoted music events on March 21, each one with text in English and Khmer. One poster featured the *Shaolin* Band and Minnesotan singer Rotana, a beautiful young woman, and a clean-cut young pop music "Super Star from Cambodia, *Sen ranut*." Presented by SAVA, the event took place at *Sompao Meas* at 450 Chelmsford St. (tickets $20 or $25 at the door). Also performing last Saturday were "two sexy stars from Seattle" at the *Pailin* Restaurant, 6 Branch St, plus the six alluring members of the H2O Band (tickets $20, food included). A third poster advertised a Khmer New Year party on Saturday, April 11, at the Lowell Elks Lodge, 40 Old Ferry Road. This is a "Charity Fundraiser for Angkor Hospital for Children" (tickets $15 or $20 at the door). The dress code: "Proper attire or your best Khmer outfit." Other notices or announcements taped on the wall ranged from census information and tax preparation services to apartments available and help wanted in a nails shop.

Customers streamed into the store all the while I was there, filling their plastic baskets with fruits, vegetables, meats, and other groceries. I bought scallions, cilantro, pickling cucumbers, and green grapes. I was reminded of my grandfather's market in Little Canada and what Saturday mornings must have been like in that ethnic enclave years ago—the special foods and local talk that come with such places. These stores are information clearinghouses, too. It's the same at the Indian grocery next to University Music off Middlesex Street. There, it's Basmati rice and Bollywood film DVDs. In Little Canada in the 1920s, it would have been *tourtieres* (meat pies) and *L'Etoile* with the news in French.

March 24, 2009

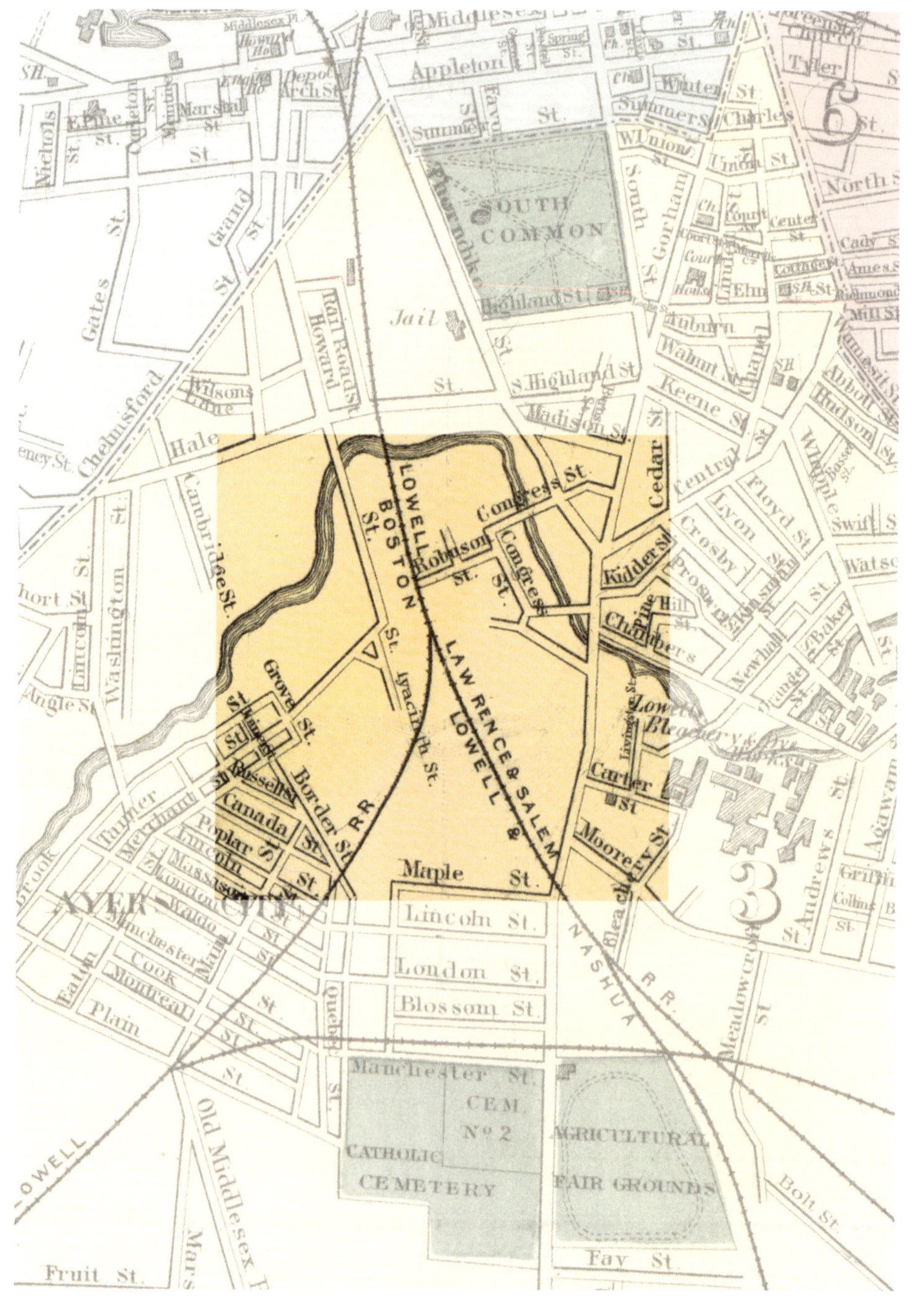

Hale-Howard Neighbors

Hood's Sarsaparilla
  Comfort Furniture
NMTW
  LRTA
Celestica
  Viewpoint
The Glory Buddhist Temple
  Buddy Elston Plumbing & Heating Supply
Clear Channel
  Sunoco
Bangkok Market
  Buck's Bar & Grill
Flanagan Square
  Bridal by Bopha
MA-COM Technology Solutions
  119 Gallery, Where Art Meets Innovation
Tepthida Khmer Cuisine
  Monro Muffler Brake & Service
7 Eleven
  Pailin Dental
Culligan Water Conditioning
  Morning Star Travel

March 25, 2009

Batman on Highland Street

A movie convoy for the boxing film *The Fighter* took over the entire front lot of the Rogers School on Highland Street across the street from where I live. The congregation of trailers, trucks, and assorted vehicles looks like a carnival round-up on Regatta Field in Pawtucketville. Security cars buzz around the long school driveway all day. Two cranes at the courthouse hold up dark screens, which I learned from Twitter reports were raised to keep the sun from blasting in the south-facing windows upstairs where scenes were being shot.

On Elm Street earlier a few residents sat on their steps, away from the stifling air inside. I asked one man if he'd seen any movie stars. He said, "I wasn't home to look—I was at the factory all day. Haven't seen any movie stars since I got home."

At the office today a colleague I've known since high school said he can't believe Hollywood is making a movie based on the experiences of the Lowell boxers. He said they couldn't put the real story on film.

Milling around the court parking area were people from the film crew, the ones whose names scroll up for minutes after the end of the film: drivers, caterers, and technicians in motion-picture craft unions.

One guy labored up the sidewalk with a pile of bottled-water cases on a handtruck. The water man is part of the team, alongside the screenwriter, personal assistants, grips, deputy cinematographer, and the woman rolling the wardrobe rack across Gorham Street. The water-guy.

In the ExtraMart gas station-and-convenience store nearby one of the clerks told me firefighters came in to get bottles of water during last week's house fire on Auburn Street, alongside the store, and at the height of the fire a firefighter hustled down the street with a case of bottled water. There are now two blackened buildings close together on Auburn.

The water-guy for the movie. He pushed the handtruck up the sidewalk from Linden to Elm St., where he stopped to light a cigarette and take a few drags before pushing the handtruck into the parking lot near the tent-covered food station.

There wasn't anything more to see, so I walked home and turned on the TV. Surfing through the channels I caught a glimpse of Mark Wahlberg making a guest appearance on the latest episode of the HBO series *Entourage*, about hungry young actors and their crew in Los Angeles, which he produces, and then on a movie channel came upon the Western *3:10 to Yuma*, starring former Dark Knight Christian Bale—the two actors who today ate lunch across the street in one of the catering stations at the Rogers School. Batman was in the gym.

April 12, 2009

NORTH COMMON
Common St.
Cross St.
Franklin St.
Cushing St.
Dutton St.
Lagrange St.
Marion St.
Cath Ch.
Market St.
Middle St.
Lowell Machine Shop
Jackson St.
Middlesex St.
Appleton St.
Summer St.
Charles St.
Union St.
North St.
SOUTH COMMON
Highland St.
Jail
Prescott Mills
Merrimack Mills
Tremont
Tilden St.
Prince St.
Cabot St.
Moody St.
Fletcher St.
Salem St.
Whiting St.
Currier Shop
Gates St.
Grand St.
Rail Road St.
Howard St.
Walnut St.
Keene St.
Madison St.
S. Highland St.
Elm St.
Tyler St.
William St.
Central St.
Lawrence St.
2
6

Scenes from a Redevelopment Zone

This morning, I went walking and looking in the area once referred to as "Uptown," but which has been recast by the city planners as the JAM (Jackson-Appleton-Middlesex) area and the adjacent in-progress Hamilton Canal District.

1. From the high ground of the Lord Overpass near Durkin's Carpeting and Interiors you see to the north the Textile Museum's white-suited astronaut reaching for a big ball of woolen yarn floating in space on that huge banner over Dutton Street. We ought to have that spaceman banner on every parking garage for a couple of months while the Museum rolls out its new permanent exhibition—*Textile Revolution: An Exploration Through Space and Time*. In a single image, the Museum pushed the dusty textile mill story into the 21st century.

2. The rocking blue graffiti letters on Sun Electric in that subterranean area off-shore of the Lord Overpass, the agitated letters on the fully painted side of the building set against a night cityscape backdrop. Electric Motors & Pumps. The left side of the mural done in peach, lavender, and greens, picking up the early spring colors, new-leafed trees, and weeds springing into shape. In the grassy path on the safe side of the guard rail the manhole cover is in synch with the theme: "Lowell Electric Light Corporation."

3. King St. Revere St. Garnet St. Middlesex St. Pearl St. Freddy's Auto Repair, Domestic and Foreign (under new management—old sign). Ocean

State Nails & Hair Salon and across the way the closed Best Buy Sea Foods (a connection?). The massive warehouse reminiscent of the former Curran-Morton behemoth on Bridge Street that was demolished to make way for Kerouac Park, an almost indestructible bunker of concrete and re-bar. U.S. Dry Cleaners. KWG PC, Computer Repairs & Sales. *La Tijera de Oro* Barbershop with its poster of artfully cut hair/shaved heads featuring tattoo-type designs, a real body-art shop. *La Differencia* Restaurant promises "The Best Caribbean Flavors." The Law Offices of George P. Jeffreys. An iron front grate pulled down tight to the sidewalk. Courthouse Deli by the Livingstone family—door propped open. Two guys eating breakfast. Construction underway at Garcia-Brogans, the Mex-Celtic eatery "getting in on the ground floor" of the Edward J. Early Jr. Garage.

4. Garrity's Antiques (Always Buying Estates). Sailboat-cover sheet music of "Bobbin' Up and Down" on a wooden table. An amateur painting of John F. Kennedy in a blue polo shirt, holding sunglasses, looking at the ocean from his Cape Cod compound. A poster from the Metropolitan Opera's 1981 production of *Parade* in N.Y. Framed Monet maritime scene print and a City of Medford Fire Department Certificate. Various lamps. A wooden sled. Trunks and chairs. Mirrors and out-of-state license plates and dishes and white figure skates. 1950s model cars. A gold metal troubadour, slightly damaged like a broken *Aphrodite*.

5. At the Lowell Transitional Living Center small clusters of people waking to the day, talking excitedly under the blooming dogwood trees. The sidewalk is a trail of pink petals. A Black man steps up and sweeps a blonde woman off her feet and into his arms with a loud "Good Morning," and everyone laughs.

6. Ever notice that the WCAP radio sign is between two signs for Cappy's Copper Kettle? WCAPPY?

7. Major's Pub. Loft 27. The Lowell Gallery. Ray Robinson's Sandwich Shoppe. Mr. Al sitting in a chair reading the paper when a Saturday morning customer steps in for a haircut. A block away at the Majestic Barbershop one guy is in a chair as two young guys wait. Washington Bank. Sim's Driving School. Electrical Distribution. The Club.

8. Garnick's Music Center. Classic used album sleeves pinned up on the side wall: *Songs by Ricky*, *The Buddy Holly Story*, *The Beatles Yesterday and Today*, *Orpheus Ascending*, *Glad All Over* by the Dave Clark Five, Elvis's *Blue Hawaii*, The Beatles' *Something New*, and *Surf City* by Jan & Dean. In the 1960s, Record Lane on Central Street and Garnick's on Middlesex were the hotspots for the latest music. Bins and bins of albums. Aisles of music in between Garnick's television sets and phonograph consoles (hi-fi and stereo). What's left is an echo of its heyday. There was a straight line to Garnick's from *J. C.'s Golden Oldies* on WLLH radio and TV's *American Bandstand, Shindig,* and *Don Kirshner's Rock Concert*.

9. Romeo and Juliet Cafe. Allied Retail Systems, Specialists in Service, Sales, and Supplies since 1959. The closed Elliot's Famous Hot Dogs stand. Cars and trucks nosed in against the Owl Diner, advertising Haddock and at least one job available. Favor Street and the Eliot Presbyterian Church. (Could they sell hot dogs on Sundays and call them Eliot's with one "l"?)

10. All the other scenes I missed.

May 9, 2009

CENTRALVILLE
MERRIMACK RIVER
CONCORD
Stackpole
Prescott Mills
Boott Mills
Massic Falls
SOUTH COMMON
Park Sq
6
2

Garden District

Up and down the narrow hilly streets that run between the Concord River and Back Central Street the green of spring is taking form in young vegetable plants, fruit tree crowns, and flower leaves. "Ali" is back in the city for a short break from his work with the State Department in Iraq, and we spent some time this morning perambulating a section of the neighborhood with many names: Chapel Hill, Back Central, Wamesit Hill, the Flats, the South End.

We checked on the progress of the grass from Father Grillo Park to Walter (Silva) Lemieux Park. We checked on the waters, from Hale Brook running swiftly through the mill cluster off Lawrence Street to the rain-fattened Concord just below Jollene Dubner Park. Two big ducks with colorful necks paddled around the bend. "Ali" said the Tigris River is not much wider than the Merrimack, at least the section near his headquarters office in Baghdad. We checked on the spiraling grapevine shoots in backyards and breezeways from New Street to North Street.

We bought cool water and imported chocolate from a Brazilian woman running a small market. She said, "The big companies are closing, but my store stays open."

"Ali" spoke to residents whom he knew from his days as a letter carrier and working for a social service agency. We talked about the defiance and hopefulness and confidence and commitment that comes with planting each seed and seedling, with trimming each vine and peach tree, with turning over the soil for another season of expected good outcomes.

We tried to notice all the handmade improvements, embellishments, and home-ly inventions that make a distinctive place—that give a particular area its special sense of place. Early in the morning people were doing yard work or cleaning the sidewalk outside their home or spraying potted plants with a hose. Regular customers bought fresh fish from the back of "John's" fish truck. We walked down social club alley (Portuguese, Lithuanian, and the Pulaski—now closed), and then cut through on a tiny street behind the courthouse to get back to our starting point.

May 16, 2009

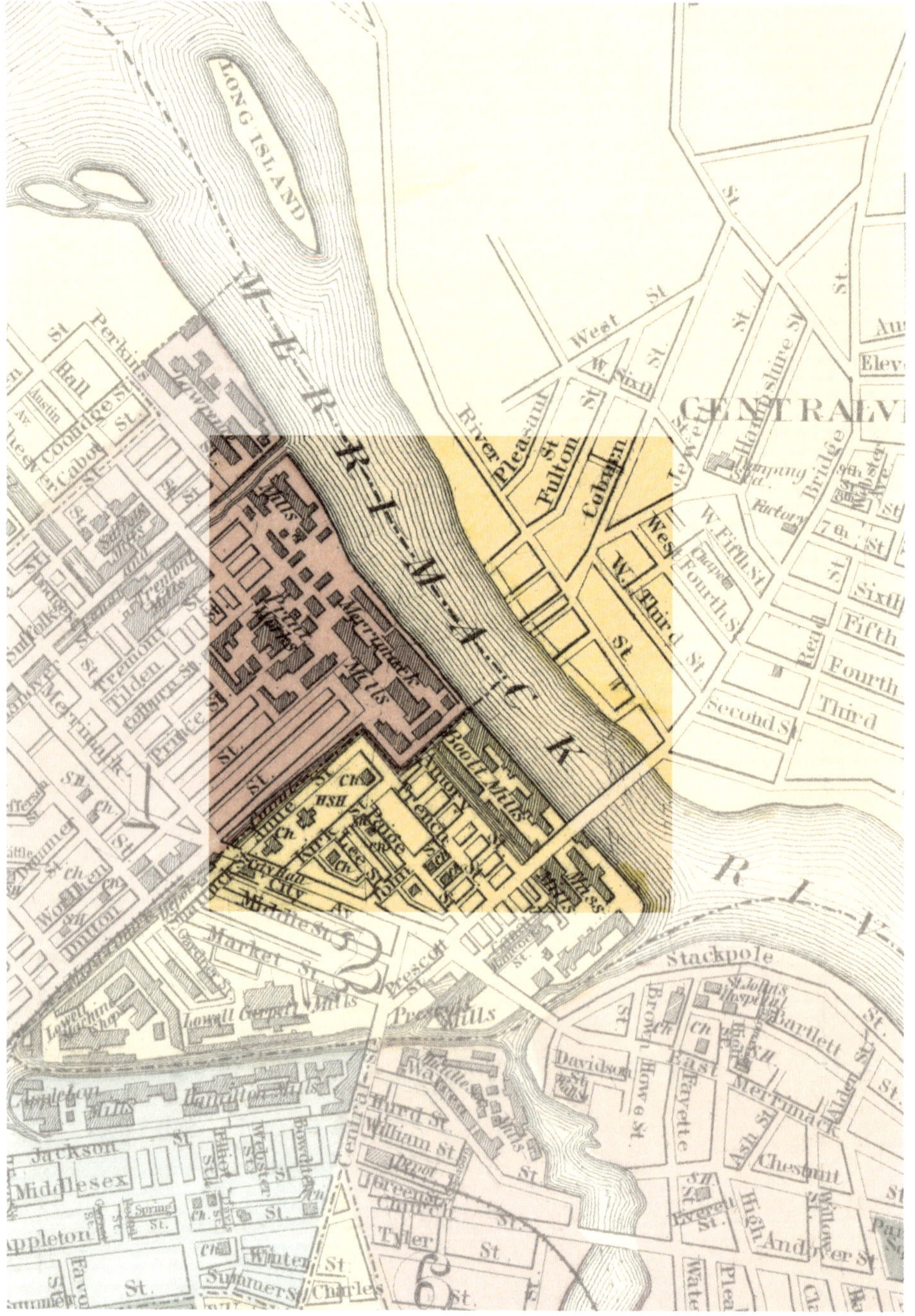

LONG ISLAND
M E R R I M A C K
R I V
West St.
Perkins
Hall
Cabot
Tremont
Tilden
Prince
Merrimack Mills
Boott Mills
River
Pleasant
Fulton
Bridge
Fifth
Fourth
Third
Second St.
Middle St.
Market St.
Prescott
Stackpole
Lowell Machine Shop
Lowell Carpet Mills
Hamilton Mills
Jackson
Middlesex
Appleton
Hurd St.
William St.
Tyler
Davidson St
East Merrimack
Bartlett
Chestnut
High
Andover St
Summer
Winter St
Charles

"I've Gone to Look for America": On Foot in a National City

New England American Studies Association Annual Meeting; "The Post-American City," October 16-18, 2009, Lowell, Mass. Friday, Oct. 16, 2009, 10:30 a.m., Boott Cotton Mills Museum, Lowell National Historical Park. "Contemporary Urban Engagements: A Panel Discussion" with Peter Taylor (UMass Boston) and John Wooding and me (UMass Lowell), moderated by Michael Millner (UMass Lowell). The following is my presentation.

In her book *The Lure of the Local*, cultural analyst Lucy Lippard writes:

> The intersection of nature, culture, history, and ideology form the ground on which we stand—our land, our place, the local. The lure of the local is the pull of the place that operates on each of us, exposing our politics and our spiritual legacies. It is the geographical component of the psychological need to belong somewhere, one antidote to a prevailing alienation.

Lowell keeps surprising me. Last month Lowell in the form of Lowell National Historical Park was selected to represent Massachusetts in a new fifty-state series of twenty-five cent coins, quarters, to be issued by the U.S. mint over the next many years, four states per year. The Lowell quarter is due in 2019. Nonetheless, it's a striking piece of news. In a public poll, Lowell National Historical Park came in second to Gloucester and its bronze Fisherman as the people's choice to represent the state. Gloucester was disqualified by the U.S.

mint because it does not have a federal historical site—national park, forest, or recreation area—which is required for the coin set. We're thirty years into the national park in Lowell and some folks still don't grasp that we are on the same list as Yellowstone, the Grand Canyon, Gettysburg, and the Statue of Liberty.

Lowell is an American icon. Any decent U.S. History textbook mentions Lowell's lead role in the emerging American Industrial Revolution, the first cluster of "high tech" in the form of power looms and integrated cloth manufacturing. And because of the National Park the city has been elevated for easier viewing and examination. Also, since 1957, when Jack Kerouac exploded like his fireworks in the literary sky, Lowell has been pulled into public view by Kerouac's trajectory—an arc across the U.S. and around the world, and across generations now.

Some people still say Lowell is the first "urban" national park, but that's not true. For example, Boston National Historical Park (1974) and Golden Gate National Recreation Area in San Francisco (1972) pre-date Lowell, established in 1978. But Lowell is distinct in that the whole city and its entire history (and pre-history) are the province of the Park rather than specific heritage sites or open spaces. Although the federal government owns only five buildings in Lowell and is active in the larger Preservation District (roughly, Downtown and the canal system), the Park Service is expected to tell the whole story of the city as a microcosm of urbanization and industrialization. I sometimes describe it as a cube of economic, social, and cultural history bounded by the city's geographic limits but unbounded in time at the bottom and top. The natural history gives us the glacier-scraped river that then gives us the human settlement; at the top it's open-ended: post-industrial, maybe post-urban, maybe post-American in the words of this gathering.

This is my place, and I'm more conscious of the National Park and city as a whole because of my work and writing. I keep looking for the "big" America that Lowell contains. I continue to be fascinated by the fact that this is my city and that it holds the place it does. My family arrived in 1880. And like a good practical New England ethnic Yankee, I think about what that means and what good it does and can do. Does that long standing require a greater responsibility on my part? The environmental magazine *Orion* this fall published a special feature about "walks" written by people from around the world. The editor says, "The walk is a universal narrative device for exploring a diverse sampling of cultures and places, ideas and environments . . . it features the movement of one or more persons on foot through a particular place and some manner of dialogue that unfolds either between characters or in the narrator's own head." I walk to try to understand the city.

Our long-ago neighbor Henry David Thoreau made much of his walking, but like a lot of other aspects of Thoreau his walking turns me off a little because he seems so intent on one-upping the next person. He boasts:

> I have met but one or two persons in the course of my life who understood the art of Walking, that is, of taking walks—who had the genius, so to speak, for sauntering, which word is beautifully derived 'from idle people who moved about the country, in the Middle Ages, and asked charity, under pretense of going *a la Sainte Terre,'* to the Holy Land . . . .

"There goes Hank again," the neighbors might have said. "He thinks he's smarter than us." Thoreau wants to engage Nature with a capital N. I want to engage the urban organism in all its parts: natural, built, and human. Thoreau seems to want to go so far into Nature that he escapes society and ultimately achieves a cosmic blend with joy-flavored, atomized plasma. Is that his transcendence? He's there, and not there. I don't want to lose touch with everything in my peripheral vision. I don't think my work here is done.

Lowell is an urban laboratory, and I'm doing things that I hope will help me understand what's really going on and what this place has to offer its inhabitants and people beyond. I've been blogging this year in an experiment in community writing. Four main contributors to a local blog, *RichardHowe.com*, are trying to capture "history as it happens" in a project called Lowell 2009. I've posted several times after taking walks in the city. But I've been writing about walking almost since I began writing poems in the mid-1970s.

I had an unexpected response to one of my walks last April, when my wife, Rosemary Noon, and I led a guided walk around Lowell's public sculpture collection. I hope you get to see a few of the ten pieces of contemporary sculpture around downtown. One of our band of walkers was Greg Page, who writes a blog called *The New Englander* (appropriate for this annual meeting). He's a civil affairs officer in the National Guard due to be deployed to Afghanistan next year. He lives downtown and embraces city life. He remarked on the impact the sculpture walk had made on him—allowing him to see things he'd missed, making "the too familiar visible," as Archibald MacLeish said Robert Frost's poetry does for us. And Greg connected the experience to his recent reading of Thomas Ricks' book about the Iraq War, *The Gamble*, in which Ricks describes the shift in policy from Secretary of Defense Donald Rumsfeld's strategy to Gen. David Petraeus' approach in 2007, summed up like this: "If you want to get to know an area and its 'human geography,' you have to get out of your vehicle and you have to walk the streets."

Greg titled his post that day, "Petraeus-Odierno Meets Marion-Noon." When we met at the National Park Visitor Center for the walk, Greg writes that "we were getting ready for a dismounted patrol on our all-weather personnel carriers—we were going on foot." I look for America when I'm out on the Lowell streets.

In his song "America," Paul Simon writes: "So we bought a pack of cigarettes, /And Mrs. Wagner's pies, /And walked off to look for America." It's the way it has happened so many times before. Native peoples wore out footpaths in the Eastern woodlands. Jack Kerouac walked off to look for America before he got in the passenger seat of a car. Thoreau "traveled widely in Concord," on foot. The pioneering families often walked behind their wagons going west. Lowell millworkers walked or promenaded along the new canals on Sunday afternoons. Sustainability advocates now talk about walkability and Active-Living cities. A quick online search brought me to neighborhood walking sites in Chicago, Fort Wayne, Albuquerque, Rochester, Valparaiso, Brooklyn, Dayton, Omaha, New Orleans, and others. With a community organizer as President, the time seems right to find where we fit on foot, to "dismount" as the soldier Greg Page writes. Maybe the post-American city is right underfoot all the time.

October 16, 2009

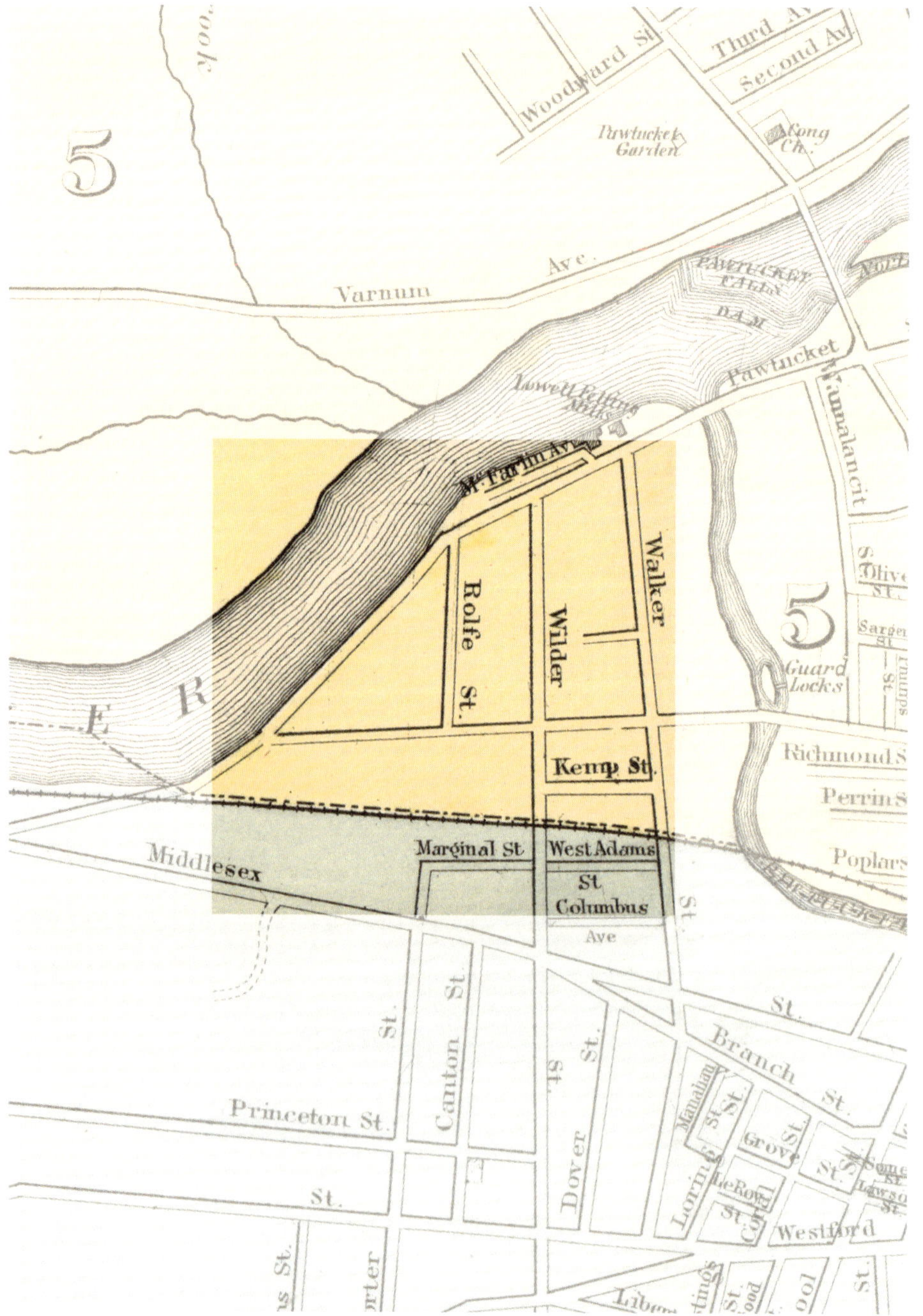

5
Woodward St
Third Av
Second Av
Pawtucket Garden
Varnum Ave.
Pawtucket Dam
Pawtucket
Lowell Felting Mills
Wannalancit
Walker
Rolfe St.
Wilder
5
Guard Locks
Kemp St.
Richmond S
Perrin S
Marginal St
West Adams St
Columbus Ave
Middlesex
Poplar S
Canton St.
Dover St.
Branch St.
Princeton St.
Grove St.
Westford

Murphy

I'm calling my latest walking report "Murphy" because in the Highlands this morning I saw several of the blue Murphy campaign signs hanging around post-election, and Patrick Murphy was on the front page of the *Sun* this morning, along with councilors-elect Franky Descoteaux and Joe Mendonca. I don't know what someone would call the area I walked with my brother early this morning, maybe the "Middle" Highlands, as opposed to the Lower Highlands or Upper Highlands. It's a neighborhood that I don't know very well. We were in the area of Penniman Circle, the new Morey School (which looks suburban), and the back side of the Wilder Street Historic District with its many well-kept Victorian-style houses.

Even in a dense residential section like this one there are institutional presences tucked between houses, including Calvary Baptist Church, Montefiore Synagogue, St. George Greek Orthodox Church, Willow Manor Nursing Home, and the school mentioned above. All within a few blocks.

We stopped at the Glacier Oval, an oddity for monuments in the city. I had not seen it up close. It's an ovoid section of ledge about twenty feet long and ten feet wide. At first, I thought a huge boulder had been sliced off, leaving a rugged layer of ancient rock, but it's a patch of ledge. Someone reading this can enlighten us about it. (I just Googled the term and got a passage from one of the books by the Old Residents Historical Association, which says it's a ledge behind the Highland Church "deeply furrowed" by the legendary "glacier.")

I was eager to walk this morning because of the mild weather on a November Sunday. Up and down the streets flowers bloomed, including lots of healthy-looking red, pink, and white roses. Some trees were leafless while others held onto their full golden crowns. A small grove of bamboo filled the corner of one yard; nearby was a large Chinese dog made of concrete. Christmas and Halloween decorations overlapped on one block.

Part of the writing impulse is the urge to name things and describe experiences, and I was thinking of that as my brother and I kicked through the leaves on the sidewalks. The colors are exceptional this year. I've been looking at the leaves up close and far away and trying to come up with words to paint the colors. From a distance, the tan leaves under the trees look like a ring of pencil shavings.

The neighborhood was waking up between 7:45 and 8:45 a.m. At the Donut Shack on Westford Street a man in slippers, pajama bottoms, and a jacket walked out with a coffee and a small bag. Most of the political signs were gone. A black-and-pink Mercier sign leaned into the shrubs in one yard. You almost wouldn't know from the streetscape there had been a big election last Tuesday. Opara signs hung in windows of a few shops. Ben O. is an African immigrant, part of a growing group in Lowell. The candidates and their supporters had cleaned up quickly.

I asked my brother to guess how many leaves were on the ground across the city. We couldn't say. Millions, hundreds of millions? Billions and billions, as Carl Sagan said about the stars? Can you count the leaves on one block and project the total number? It's a lot of biomass, as they say.

November 8, 2009

NORTH COMMON
Common St.
Market
Merrimack
Tremont
Tilden
Prince
Adams
Fenwick St.
Butterfield St.
Cross St.
Marion
Lagrange
Franklin St.
Cushing St.
Dutton St.
Western Av.
Currier Shop
Gas Works
Middle St.
Market St.
Prescott
Lowell Machine Shops
Appleton Mills
Hamilton
Jackson
Middlesex
Middlesex Pl.
Appleton
Depot
Arch St.
Summer St.
Favor St.
Spring St.
Winter St.
Summer St.
W. Union
South St.
Gorham
SOUTH COMMON
Thorndike
Highland St.
Charles
Union St.
Central
William St.
Tyler
North St.
Nichols
Marshall
Grand St.
Gates St.
Chelmsford
Jail
Howard
Rail Road St.
S. Highland St.
Auburn
Walnut
Keene St.
Madison St.
Hale
Cedar St.
Chapel
Floyd St.
Lyon
Crosby
Congress St.
Robinson
LOWELL
BOSTON
LAW
Cambridge St.
Washington
Lincoln
Short St.
Kidder St.
Chambers
Pine Hill
Newhall
Whipple
Abbott
Hudson
Swift
Watson
Baker
Elm
Court
Center
Cady St.
Ames St.
Wilsons Lane

Two Hearts Café, Badfinger & a Raspberry Lime Rickey

I hiked in the immediate neighborhood this afternoon, from the JAM district (Jackson-Appleton-Middlesex streets) to the edge of Back Central and back to the South Common Historic District where my family lives. I'd been meaning to go to the Brazilian "bakery & eatery" on Appleton in the former New York Nails shop across from Store 24. The miniature brick building houses Two Hearts Café, which offers cakes, coffee, catering, specialty Brazilian pastries, and breads. I'm going back tomorrow morning to pick up a few fresh items to take to a breakfast with friends. Everything looks good. The place is open long hours—weekdays as early as 5:30 a.m.

My next stop was Garnick's Music emporium at 54 Middlesex Street, which is practically an institution for its longevity. Owner Bob Garnick watched the record industry rocket to the moon in the '60s, fall to Earth with the coming of the Internet, and now transform itself so that he is selling more albums on the 'net these days than product out of the store. He says the young customers want the original vinyl recordings of The Beatles, Dylan, Rolling Stones, Hendrix, and other classic artists. The store today has bins and bins of compact discs (new and used) and albums of hundreds of artists. The place is like an archive of musical history. Thanks to Bob's heavy ordering hand back in the day, he has a massive inventory of just what new consumers and collector-types want. Someone said if you stay in one place long enough the whole world comes to you.

I've been humming the 1970 hit "No Matter What" ever since Marc Cohn played his version of the song at Boarding House Park downtown a few weeks ago. I asked Bob what he had in stock for Badfinger CDs. In a minute he had in his hand two from the "new" section: *No Dice* (1970), which includes "No Matter What," features the memorable alluring fashion model Kathy, one name only, in silver tones gesturing come-hither on the album cover; and *Straight Up* (1972), with the now golden-oldies "Baby Blue" and "Day After Day." George Harrison discovered Badfinger for Apple Records and produced several tracks on *Straight Up*, including "Day After Day," on which he plays slide guitar. I would've preferred a "best of" collection that included Badfinger's other giant hit, "Come and Get It," but Bob made me a nice offer for the two CDs, plus today is a sales-tax-free day.

At Danas' Luncheonette, 62 Gorham Street, at the corner where Central, Gorham, Appleton, and Church streets converge, Peter Danas recently completed repairs to the front of the store caved in by a crashing car. I hadn't seen Peter for a while and don't stop in often enough, so I was glad to find the door still open after 5 p.m. He was wrapping up but insisted that I have one of the famous raspberry lime rickey drinks whose mixture he has perfected over the years. I was refreshed. Peter's a writer, too. His poem about St. Peter Church, the size of a small cathedral, which long stood up the street before being closed and then demolished by the bishop, is printed on a large poster on the back wall. Danas Fruit and Confectionery—the full name—sells sandwiches, homemade candies, and old-fashioned ice cream counter specials. Peter's known for the abundant fruit baskets that the family assembles and ships around the country. Piles of green apples, bananas, oranges, and pears with cookies, crackers, and cheese stuck in between.

The building drips character, which was not missed by location scouts for the film *School Ties* in 1992. Scenes were shot in the store and the alley on the side with a cast of emerging stars: Brendan Fraser, Matt Damon, Ben Affleck, Amy Locane, Chris O'Donnell, and others. Familiar locals made it to the final cut as extras and glided over a red carpet for the hometown opening.

August 14, 2010

5
Guard Locks
Oliver St.
Sargent St
Phillips St.
School
Varney
Butterfield St.
CH
Cross St.
North Common
Common St.
Adams
Fenwick St.
Cath Ch
Broadway
Richmond St.
Kemp St.
Perrin St.
Mach Shop
Fact'y
Currier Shop
Rock
Franklin
Lagrange
Marion
Poplar St
Gas Works
Western Av.
Cushing St.
Dutton St.
West Adams St
Columbus Ave
Rolfe St.
Wilder
Walker St.
Dover St.
Branch St.
Manahan St.
Grove St.
Cemetery No 1
S.H.
Somerset St.
Lawson St.
LeRoy St
Loring
Westford
Nichols St.
E. Pine St.
Carleton St.
Marshall St.
Middlesex Pl.
Howard Ho.
Depot
Arch St.
Liberty
Hastings St.
Osgood St.
School St.
Lane St.
Horn St.
Smith St.
Gates St.
Grand St.
Rail Road St.
Howard
Wilsons Lane
Hale
Chelmsford
Barclay St.
Cheney St.
Cambridge St.
LOWELL
HIGHLANDS
4
Shaw St.
Tannery
New Fletcher St.
Short St.
B. St.
Lombard
Gold
Mt Vernon St.
Bowers St.
Fletcher
Hancock Ave
Clark St.

Grand Street Peace Walk

Standing on the old Armory site on Westford Street just beyond the Lord Overpass with about sixty people at 2:00 p.m., I couldn't help thinking that Armory Park was being used for another kind of conflict, even war in the broadest sense—a war against violence like the war against poverty championed by Rev. Dr. Martin Luther King, Jr., whom we'll be remembering and honoring in two weeks.

Taya Dixon Mullane of the Lower Highlands Neighborhood Group (LHNG) called everyone into a loose circle and said a few words, offering condolences to the families of Corinna Ouer, the young woman who was killed yesterday on Grand Street, and the other young people who were shot and wounded in an attack at a house party nearby. Captain Kevin Sullivan, commander of the district's police activities, spoke about the senselessness of the shootings and the daily efforts of City police to keep the peace. He praised neighborhood leaders and encouraged everyone to increase their involvement in neighborhood issues. He noted the diversity of the group, people from all backgrounds and heritages, a good sign.

Mayor Jim Milinazzo offered sympathy to the families and friends of the victims on behalf of the residents of Lowell and his colleagues on the City Council. Greg Croteau of the United Teen Equality Center spoke briefly about UTEC's effort to prevent violence and engage youth in positive ways. Artists Walter and Marianne of 119 Gallery at the corner of Chelmsford Street and Grand stood with their neighbors. I saw other familiar faces in the crowd.

The LHNG distributed strips of long wide purple ribbon for people to tie to utility poles and street posts, a symbol of respect and remembrance. A police car with whirling blue lights crawled ahead of the procession and stopped in front of the house where shots had been fired. Several young people who know the victims tied ribbons on the iron railings on both sides of the front stairs of the white duplex. A man wearing a white dust mask kept up his work, carrying plastic bags of something out of the basement of the house. People watched from porches and windows in homes up and down the street. When we passed the Bethel AME Church, everyone heard the live music inside. Somebody was playing drums. Light rain fell on the marchers.

January 2, 2011

Perkins
Hall
Cabot
St.
Tremont
Tilden
Prince St.
Merrimack
Suffolk
West
W. Sixth
CENTRALV
River
Pleasant
Fulton
Colburn
Hampshire St.
Bridge
Factory
W. Fifth St.
West Fourth St.
W. Third St.
Chapel
Sixth
Fifth
Fourth
Third
Second St.
Booth Mills
Merrimack Mills
Anne St.
Kirk
Lee St.
Paige
Ch.
HSH
City Hall
City Av.
Middle St.
Market St.
Prescott St.
Prescott Mills
Lowell Carpet Mills
Lowell Machine Shop
Central St.
2
1
6
Stackpole
St. Johns Hospital
Bartlett
Brown
Howe St.
Davidson St.
East Merrimack
Fayette
Ash St.
Alder St.
Chestnut
Appleton Mills
Hamilton Mills
Jackson
Middlesex
Appleton
Hurd St.
William St.
Depot
Green St.
Church
Tyler
St.
Elliot
Webster
Bowden
Spring
Winter St.
Summer St.
Charles
W. Union
Union St.
North St.
Everett St.
High
Andover St.
Water
Pleasant St.
Willow
Clay St.
Harrison
Pond St.
Oak St.
SOUTH COMMON
Thorndike
Highland St.
South
Gorham
Court
Center St.
Cottage St.
Cady St.
Ames St.
Elm
Richmond
Mill St.
Auburn
Lawrence
Massic Falls

Tom & Me

Arthur's Paradise Diner is tucked in along the canal in the shadow of the Boott Cotton Mills. Eating there is like eating inside an old wooden toolbox that is perfectly designed, without an inch of wasted space between the griddle and the booths. Tom ordered the cheese omelet and gave in to the cook's urging to have just a minor pile of home fries while I chose the "small" French toast breakfast (That's three pieces for small; the large is six, can you believe it?) with potatoes on the side, which I didn't finish. Tom said he hadn't eaten in the diner since high school. I don't imagine the decor has changed much since the late '50s. The place was busy on Saturday morning even though Bridge Street was quiet at 8.15 a.m. It was a good morning for a walk.

From the diner we headed up the Eastern Canal with the sun at our backs, admiring the craftsmanship in the preservation work and new construction at the Boott, the restored boarding house (Mogan Cultural Center), not-so-new Boarding House Park pergola/performance pavilion, Robert Cumming's three-part sculpture, Canalway path and railings, all the improvements in the area that says "National Park" more than any other except for the Lower Locks Complex between Middlesex Community College's main building and the UMass Lowell Inn & Conference Center (ICC). Tom recounted stories of his extended family that are filled with enough drama for a family saga trilogy. You don't have to be Shakespeare to see the drama in your driveway.

We crossed French Street at Lucy Larcom Park and paid our respects to the poet, editor, teacher, abolitionist who had her own park before Jack K. got his in 1988. Ellen Rothenberg's serial public art installation in the park includes an unforgettable quote from Sarah Bagley, editor of the fiery *Voice of Industry* pro-labor newspaper of the 1840s: "Truth loses nothing upon investigation." That would be a good slogan for a politician trying to beat back opponents who treat facts like a twistie used to tie up the bread bag. Apparently, no photo or illustration of Sarah Bagley exists. She was a pioneer among women working beyond the farm and village and became the first female telegraph operator of her day.

Our path turned up Merrimack Street, through Monument Square and the Ladd & Whitney Civil War tribute (Luther Ladd was seventeen years old when he was killed on the street in Baltimore on his way to help protect Washington, D.C.) We stopped to take a good look at the Smith Baker Center, whose exterior red glowed in the early morning sun. I told Tom about the plans for the Kerouac Creativity Center and the prospects for a high-energy community arts program in the building. He liked the location, right across the street from Pollard Memorial Library and City Hall, and within sight of the Whistler House Museum of Art. We kept going up Merrimack, where he pointed out the same liquor store that sold him beer when he was in high school and way under twenty-one. He said he had heard from someone that the pizza is tasty at Brothers Pizza at the corner of Cabot and Merrimack. We cut up Cabot and curled back on Market, passing the *Club des Citoyens Americains,* one of the stalwart social clubs that dot the city. It strikes me that most of these gathering places are primed for a generational turn. Maybe with an influx of new members these clubs can be re-energized as the vital "third places" that younger Lowellians say they are looking for.

When we got to Nick's barbershop across from North Common Village, the owner I presume was dozing in one of the swivel chairs. Somebody has got to document this fantastic shop in photographs and/or video while it has its amazing interior. The walls are completely adorned with posters, snapshots, Polaroids, news clippings, tickets, stickers, you name it. No fine artist could do a better job with an installation evoking time and place and culture. There's a strong Sinatra thread, but so much more. It's a time machine and wall-mounted archive. My friends at the National Park Service should certify this as a historical site and work with the owner to save it as is to show what Lowell culture is like in this long moment. And let the haircuts continue.

We crossed Market and stepped behind one of the brick housing units at North Common Village to get in back of Holy Trinity Church, where there was still a topping of snow on the faux temple ruins in the newly landscaped and paved parking lot. From there we headed toward the Whistler House Museum, which has a Lowell-theme art exhibition this month. The opening reception is next Saturday. Tom said he'd wander back in the afternoon to see the show.

We looped back on Dutton and turned south on Market to get back to the ICC where he is staying. Tom said the downtown looks wonderful compared to the business sector he had driven through on Rte. 38, going from Lowell to Tewksbury the day before. He said that mishmash of commercial sites, shopping strip, parking-lot heavy parcels, fast food drive-thru's, and auto service outfits of all kinds reminded him of nothing so much as Wasilla, Alaska, home of she-who-must-be-heard. Although he winters in Maine now, Tom's permanent address is still Alaska, and he has his own view of what you can see from there.

April 3, 2011

More from the Streets

Merrimack Street

Anyone who's been here long enough has had an hour like this. Streets about empty, air not hot, not cold. It could be a Sunday morning or a Wednesday evening, or any day after work, but not right after the office closes, maybe you stay to check the headlines.

The place yours for once, or again, you walk down Merrimack, past Jordan's minimalist window dressing, one black torso filling a yellow sweater, and the CVS, door open, scent of candy and medicine, past Cherry's, the mankins severe, past Prince's books, and the shoe store, all those objects behind plate glass creating a museum of the ordinary. The entire street is the Mundane Institute, commerce having surrendered at 5 p.m. as the human push changed direction.

There's no ambition in things. This is the moment to look. With no merchant presenting it, the shoe is like a flower, a stone. Farther on, the landmark clock in the Square and SUN Building, for years the closest thing to a skyscraper—across the street, Meehan Tours, Christian Science Reading Room, then the murky canal under the bridge and hissing pipe by the railing.

The Auditorium and Massachusetts Mills over there, and to the right, beyond the parking lot, what's left of the Strand, which featured *A Hard Day's Night* almost twenty years ago. At this hour, I know the meaning of familiar, know this is where I am and know some of what was, what is, and where Bridge Street goes, but still know so little, no knowing the other stories.

1983

Labor Day Eve

Began at H&H Paper, ex-boarding house for mill hands, in blueprints as a cultural center, then headed to the Boott Mills yard, the bell tower with shuttle weathervane an exclamation mark on a brick cliff. Near the gate, a Locks & Canals truck.

Crossed French Street to John Street, passing the Trade School and double-deck car lot's wrap-around mural: the mass production of textiles, from enslaved cotton pickers to modern strike banners to the river that juiced the looms.

Behind the five-and-dime stores, I stopped at an empty lot, once a bar. At times in the '50s, when my father was laid-off from work at his mill and I was too young for school, we'd drive Mum downtown to the women's clothing store where she worked. We'd get a booth in the bar, order a beer from him and an orangeade for me, and go back home.

Around the corner, one building rules Kearney Square, named for a World War I soldier. With its ten stories, the SUN dazzled in 1914. The lighted roof signs stayed when the newspaper moved. Electric SUN, each night a contradiction, a message, prayer, torch, fist, business card above Lowell chimneys. From Centralville across the river, it's blue. From the North Common side SUN glows red.

Turned up Merrimack, looking towards City Hall, civic temple, clean angles backed by sky, spread eagle crowning tip-top gold ball, time hands correct on the tower's large clock face. Near St. Anne's Episcopal Church, in Lucy Larcom Park, grass strip named for the so-called "mill girl poet," who was an abolitionist, editor, memoir author, a Kids' Fair was breaking camp, the clowns, sheep, popcorn vendor, even Santa Claus, all set to leave.

On cobbled Shattuck Street, outside my office, *Lowell Historic Preservation Commission, U.S. Department of the Interior*, I paused, thinking, "I work at a government desk. The United States of America pays me to remember." Where I've eaten junk, hugged girls, spent money, there, and there, on sidewalks unclaimed by the famous, any number of persons have stood in the weather, answering the clock, the bell.

1984

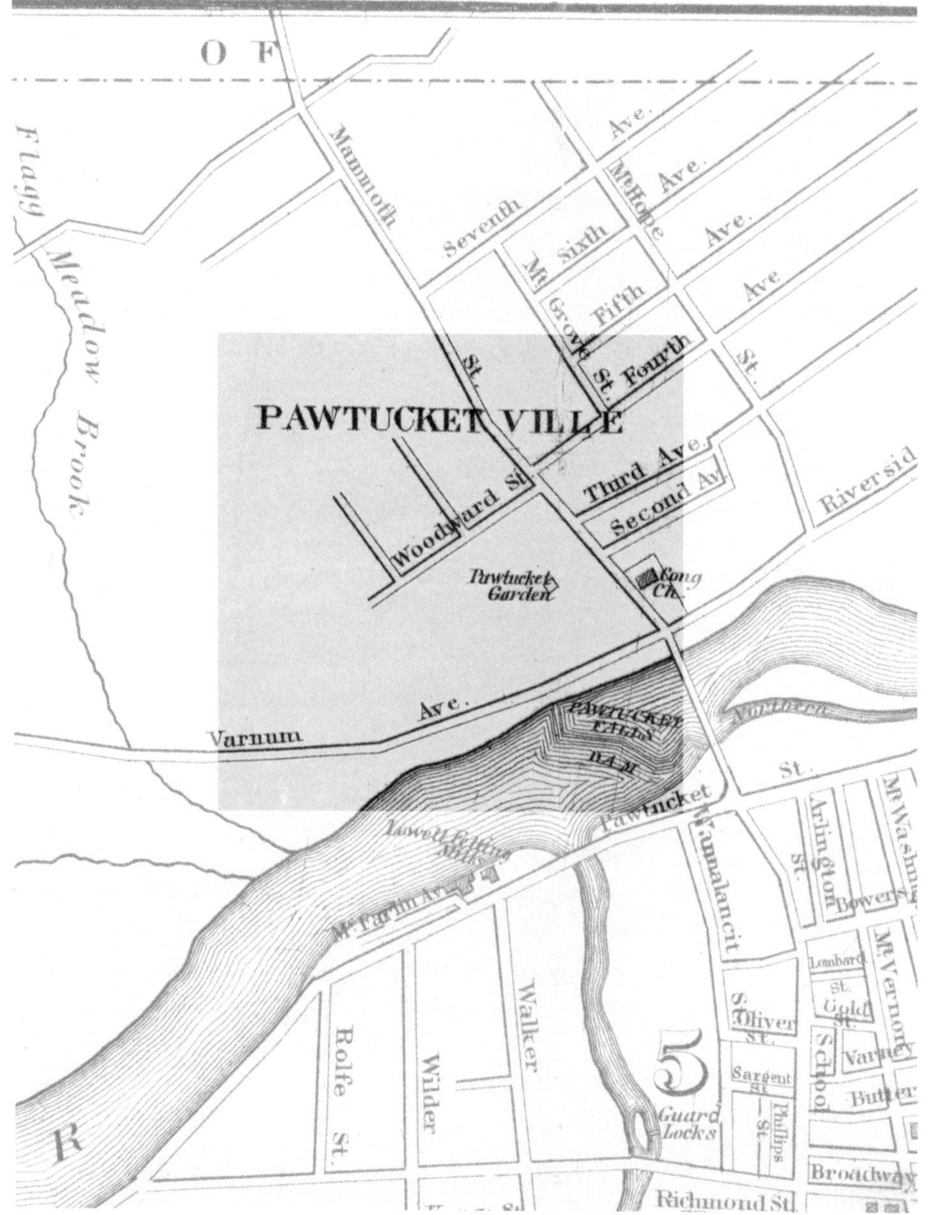

O F
Flagg
Meadow Brook
Mammoth
St.
Seventh
Ave.
Mt. Hope
Sixth
Fifth
Fourth
Mt. Grove St.
St.
PAWTUCKET VILLE
Third Ave.
Second Av
Woodward St.
Riversid
Pawtucket Garden
Cong. Ch.
Varnum
Ave.
PAWTUCKET FALLS DAM
Northern
St.
Pawtucket
Wannalancit
Arlington St.
Bowers
Lowell Felting Mills
McFarlin Ave.
Lombard St.
Mt. Vernon
Gold St.
Oliver St.
School
Varney
Sargent St.
Phillips St.
Butter
Walker
Wilder
Rolfe St.
5
Guard Locks
Broadway
Richmond St.
R

Mammoth Road

Rusty tin lids, cloth scraps, newspaper pages, a penny,
bits of metal, a kid's sneaker, gum wrappers, cigarette butts,
a roach clip, a slipper, one black rubber boot, broken pencils,
rain-scarred magazine pages, flat gold aluminum beer cans,
green glass, labels, a blue ballpoint pen, hunks of wood,
weeds, crinkled cigarette packs, empty matchbooks, tinfoil,
torn Rice Krispies box, screw-off caps, twist-off bottle tops,
two creased baseball cards, flat orange juice carton,
red bike reflector, corroded tail pipe, Styrofoam coffee cup,
plastic six-pack holders, brown beer bottles, tonic cans
(Tab, Sprite, 7-Up, Diet Pepsi, Fresca, Mountain Dew), a dog chew,
black electrical tape, a 6.5-ounce Coke bottle from Albany, N.Y.,
red-and-white straws, temperature knob printed Hot Warm Normal.

1985

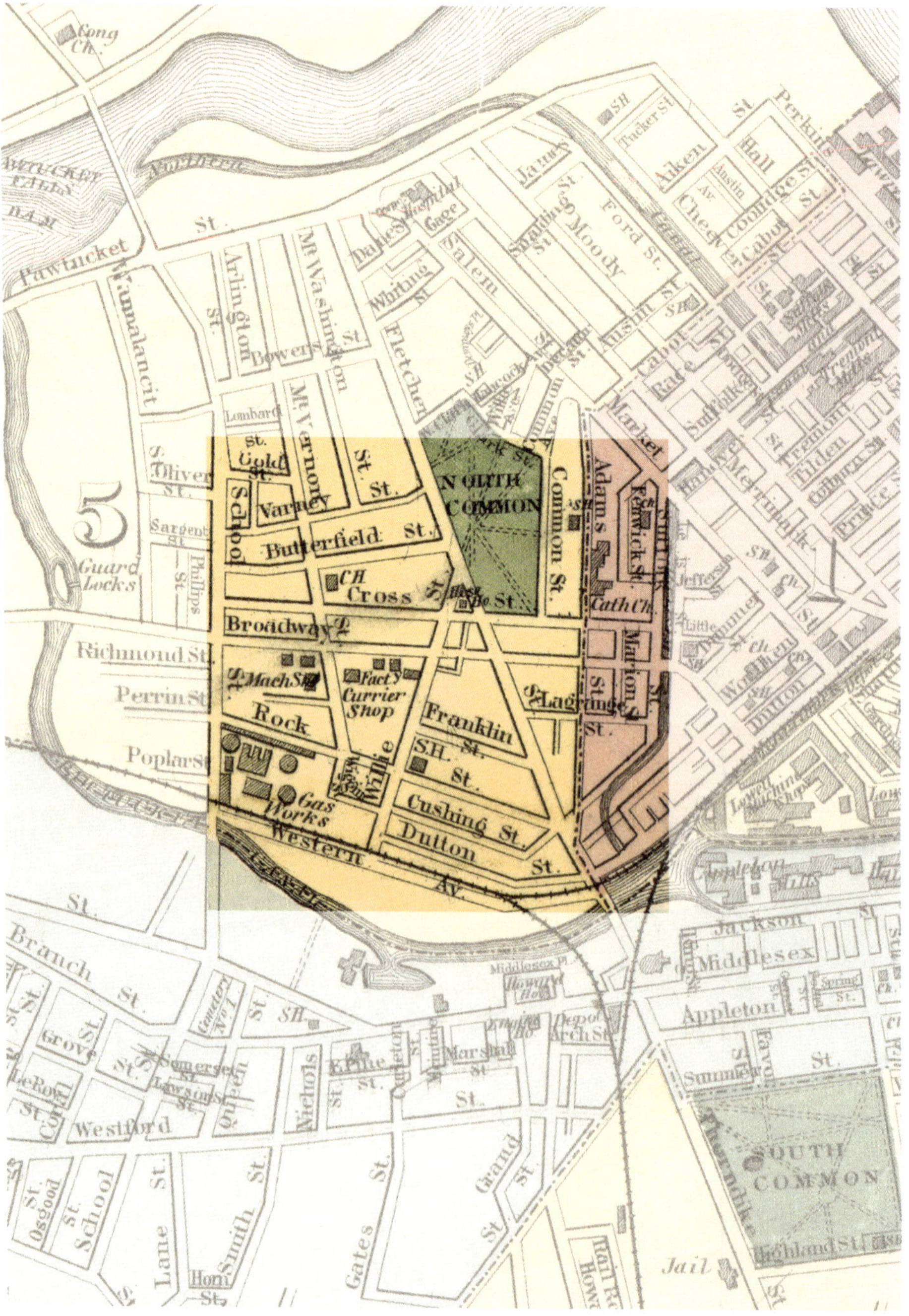

NORTH COMMON
SOUTH COMMON
Pawtucket St.
Broadway St.
Butterfield St.
Cross St.
Franklin St.
Cushing St.
Dutton St.
Western Av.
Rock St.
Gas Works
Common St.
Adams St.
Marion St.
Lagrange St.
Richmond St.
Perrin St.
Poplar St.
Guard Locks
Middlesex
Appleton St.
Jackson
Westford
Jail

A Higher Level of Notation

"If astronomy teaches us anything, it teaches that man is but a detail in the evolution of the Universe, and that resemblant though diverse details are inevitably to be expected in the host of orbs around him. He learns that though he will probably never find his double anywhere, he is destined to discover any number of cousins scattered through space."—Percival Lowell, astronomer, 1895

On Sunday morning the streets are wider, quiet, like the sky-colored river. There's a rest in the song, a pause in the working rhythm. It's a chance to look hard, to see what can be seen, to find what can be found.

Rolling down Salem and Market streets, radio tuned to "Greek Melodies," on WLLH, I feel the layers of occupation. The matching weights of St. Patrick's and gold-capped Holy Trinity pin down the Acre neighborhood for good. Like another Ellis Island, this parcel bears tracks of those who have carried on. Signs make an Embassy Row: *Club des Citoyens Americains*, Olympia, Phnom Penh.

The overlay sticks, links up in a set. The census schedule is richer. The truth hits home as my eye catches gallon cans of olive oil gleaming in the window of an orange storefront. Men haul sacks of rice. An old man crossing Worthen Street walks his dog toward the big brick mill. He stands for all scarred and decorated survivors, plus their line of makers.

From a third story porch somebody's aunt looks for Marion's Meat Market, a place that was erased like the wrong price on a grocery bill in Little Canada. At a stop sign I check the rearview mirror, trying to stitch together in a moment more than a century-and-a-half of life lived under a title, a surname, "that great fact we call Lowell." A name layered over tribal place names.

I try to retain what I'm told, but the brain is weaker than I'd like. I'm glad that remnants can be triggers and grateful for discovery through preservation, for the texture of diversity, this stained-glass history. Looking back and looking at, I see the pattern is a turn, with each turn wheeling in a world colored by long gone motions.

Our culture, the social protoplasm in which we love, work, dream, stirred by all this turning, animates each frame. We are what we were as much as what we are. What we will become is in part our choice. We can always change and change again.

1986

Notes

Hale-Howard Neighbors: Hale and Howard streets in the Lower Highlands neighborhood of Lowell were the hub of an area across the tracks from the city's train station. This long-settled part of the community had many Jewish, Black, and Puerto Rican families, as well as small businesses and two synagogues. "Hale-Howard" was marked for "urban renewal" in the 1970s, a time when that public policy term meant removal of residents, demolition of old structures, and promised redevelopment. Once cleared, there was some industrial development, but no new housing as originally planned. In recent decades many Southeast Asian families have moved into the area. Glory Temple serves the Buddhist believers. (Credit to DIY Lowell on the web for background information)

Batman on Highland Street: The 2010 film *The Fighter* is the story of Lowell boxers Micky Ward, a one-time champion, and his troubled half-brother Dicky Ecklund as they navigate the tough sports world from their hometown to a title match in London. Mark Wahlberg and Christian Bale perform as the brothers. Bale and Melissa Leo in the role of Micky's girlfriend Charlene Fleming won Academy Awards for their supporting parts in the movie.

Tom & Me: Tom Sexton (1940-2025) grew up in Lowell and with his wife, Sharyn, spent most of his life in Alaska. He taught literature and writing at the University of Alaska, Anchorage, and co-founded *The Alaska Quarterly Review.* He published eighteen collections of poetry and served a term as Poet Laureate of Alaska. Among his books are three volumes of Lowell poems: *A Clock with No Hands, Bridge Street at Dusk,* and *Cummiskey Alley.* About his admired poems about the ancient Chinese poets and nature in North America, the *New York Times Book Review* writes: "He revels in the natural: river otters and Arctic char, sedge wrens and yellow warblers, witch hazel and the wolves of Denali."

A Higher Level of Notation: Composed in my head while driving. For further background, see my note in the acknowledgments on the copyright page.

ENTERING
INC.
1826
LOWELL

Appendix: Lowell Walks

Lowell Walks was founded by Richard P. Howe Jr. in 2015. A series of free, ninety-minute guided walks of downtown Lowell, each led by a different volunteer guide, Lowell Walks averaged one hundred people per walk. Most of the walks began at 10 a.m. on a Saturday morning at the Lowell National Historical Park Visitor Center at 246 Market Street. Besides informing participants of interesting facets of Lowell history, the walks promoted downtown businesses, strengthened a sense of community, and created momentum to make the city a more walkable place.

Around 2010, Dick Howe signed on to assist local historian Catherine Goodwin, who led tours at the Lowell Cemetery for some thirty years. Prior to launching Lowell Walks, he had given sixty cemetery tours for groups ranging from ten people to one hundred and twenty. From this experience he says he learned that people love good stories, no matter the topic, as long as the presenter is engaging and interesting. He believes that the thought- and feeling-provoking information taps into something in the core of each human being. He adds, "Nothing can replace being on the ground, standing shoulder-to-shoulder with other people when you hear a compelling story. I'm a huge proponent of social media, video, and the Internet, but there is no substitute for seeing, hearing, smelling, and feeling an actual place."

Below is a list of past Lowell Walks, showing the title of the tour, name of the tour guide, and when available the number of people who participated:

2015

1. The Lowell Public Art Collection with cultural advocates Rosemary Noon & Paul Marion (107)
2. Literary Lowell & Pollard Library with librarian Sean Thibodeau (76)
3. Triumphs of Preservation with developer Fred Faust (81)
4. Hamilton Canal District with City planner Allison Lamey (129)
5. Inside Lowell High School with former Headmaster Brian Martin (86)
6. Trains & Trolleys in Lowell with planner Christopher Hayes (120)
7. Irish in the Acre with historian Dave McKean (125)
8. Abolitionists in Lowell with historian Bob Forrant (119)

9. Natural Lowell with Jane Calvin, executive director, Lowell Parks & Conservation Trust (75)
10. Green Buildings in Lowell with architect Jay Mason (43)
11. Artists Past & Present with arts leader Jim Dyment (86)
12. Renewing the Acre with neighborhood leader Dave Ouellette (105)
13. Lowell Monuments with historian Dick Howe (167)
14: Cambodia Town with activist Ratha Paul Yem (attendance unavailable)

2016

1. Preservation Success Stories with developer Fred Faust (110)
2. Hamilton Canal Update with planner Craig Thomas (105)
3. Irish in the Acre with historian Dave McKean (115)
4. Literary Lowell with librarian Sean Thibodeau (105)
5. Upper Merrimack Street with Yun-Ju Choi, executive director, Coalition for a Better Acre (88)
6. Major Downtown Fires with Fire Dept. Captain Jason Strunk (98)
7. Public Art with cultural advocates Rosemary Noon & Paul Marion (70)
8. The Greek Acre with State Sen. Steven C. Panagiotakos (109)
9. East Merrimack Street with Dick Howe (90)
10. Lowell National Historical Park with National Park Supt. Celeste Bernardo (135)

2017

1. The Western Canal with historian Dick Howe (150)
2. Abolitionism in Lowell with historians Bob Forrant & Emily Yunes (226)
3. Churches, Art & Architecture with historian Dave McKean & Rosemary Noon (111)
4. Lowell Poets with writer Paul Marion (84)
5. Jack Kerouac's Downtown with librarian Sean Thibodeau & Kerouac scholar Roger Brunelle (96)
6. Lowell Fires with Fire Dept. Captain Jason Strunk (98)
7. Northern Canal Urban Renewal with activists Chris Hayes & Aurora Erickson (90)
8. The Hamilton Canal District with City planner Claire Ricker (110)
9. Public Health with Sue Levine & Clare Gunther, Lowell Community Health Center (50)
10. Mill Girls of Lowell with Park Ranger Tess Shatzer (105)

2018

The format of Lowell Walks changed slightly in 2018 with UMass Lowell History Professor Robert Forrant organizing and conducting four of the tours and personnel of Lowell National Historical Park organizing another. Following is a list published at the start of the season. Attendance numbers are not available.

June 23: City Hall & Pollard Memorial Library with librarian Sean Thibodeau
June 30: Infamous Lowell Crimes with activists Kerry Regan Jenness & Wayne Jenness
July 14: Downtown Architecture with Steve Stowell, director, Lowell Historic Board
July 21: Moody Street with historian Dick Howe & Coalition for a Better Acre staff
Aug 11: Galleries & Cultural Places with Liz Stewart, Cultural Organization of Lowell
Aug 25: Hamilton Canal District Update with City planner Claire Ricker
Sept 1: Lowell in World War One with Dick Howe

Spring and Summer Walks:
Saturday, April 28 and Sunday, April 29: City Hall Monuments with historian Dick Howe. These walks were part of the Lowell Arts Week celebration.
Friday, May 11 and Saturday, May 12: Lowell Cemetery Tour with Dick Howe
June 9: Lowell National Historical Park 40th Birthday Walk
June 16: Abolitionism in Lowell with historian Bob Forrant
July 7: Little Canada with Bob Forrant
Aug 18: The Immigration Experience with Bob Forrant
Sept 8: Lowell Labor History with Bob Forrant

2019

Dick Howe was unavailable for most of 2019, so only one Lowell Walk was held.
Oct 12: Benjamin F. Butler: General, Governor, Industrialist with Bob Forrant & Dick Howe

2020

Lowell Walks underwent a major reorganization for 2020 with Lowell National Historical Park assuming administrative control of the walks. An impressive schedule of twenty-five walks was created, however, due to the Covid-19 pandemic, only the first, on Women's Activism, was conducted on March 7. Community activists Resi Polixa, Allison Horrocks, Anne Mulvey, and Sheri Denk led the tour.

The author walking on Jackson Street in Lowell, 2015.

About the Author

Paul Marion (b. 1954) is the author of *Union River: Poems and Sketches* and *Lockdown Letters & Other Poems* and editor of Jack Kerouac's early writing, *Atop an Underwood* (English, French, and Italian editions). His *Mill Power* chronicles the modern revival of the historic textile factory city in which he was born, Lowell, Massachusetts. His most recent book is *Portraits Along the Way: 1976-2024*, a compilation of more than fifty profiles of people he has met in person or encountered in books, on stages, in history or otherwise, some of them public figures and others who are not household names.

His work has appeared in *Alaska Quarterly Review, The Café Review, The Massachusetts Review*, *Wisconsin Review*, *Yankee Magazine*, *Cholla Needles*, *So It Goes*, and *poetsreadingthenews.com*, as well as in anthologies and other literary magazines in the U.S., Canada, Japan, and England. He is featured in *The Grifter, the Poet, and the Runaway Train: Stories from a* Yankee *Writer's Notebook* by Geoffrey Douglas.

He is a graduate of the University of Massachusetts, Lowell, and studied in the MFA Program in Writing at the University of California, Irvine. His career work involved communications and cultural affairs in state and federal government positions.

In 1978, he founded a small publishing company, Loom Press, which has released more than sixty titles: fiction, nonfiction, poetry, photography, and anthologies.

He lives in Amesbury in the Merrimack River Valley of Massachusetts.

NO LEFT TURN
SUMMER ST
MARKO'S

New Field Notes

New Field Notes

New Field Notes

New Field Notes

New Field Notes

New Field Notes